Hooked
on
WOOL

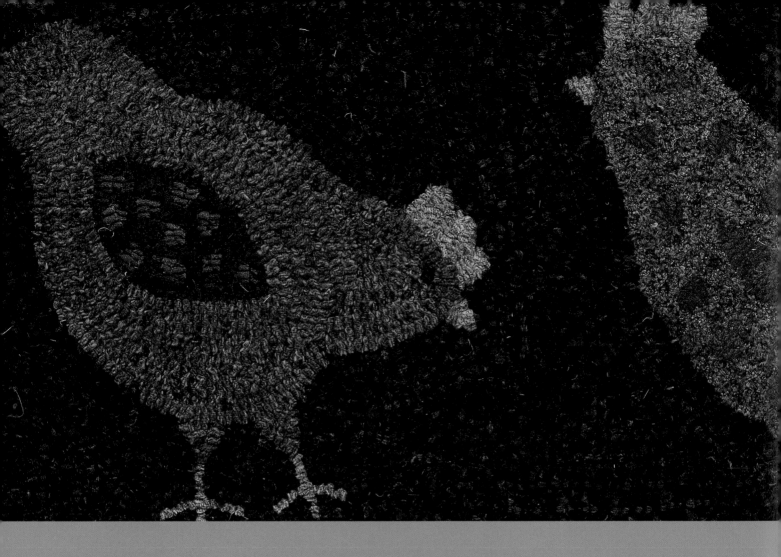

Martingale® & COMPANY

Hooked on
WOOL
Rugs, Quilts, and More

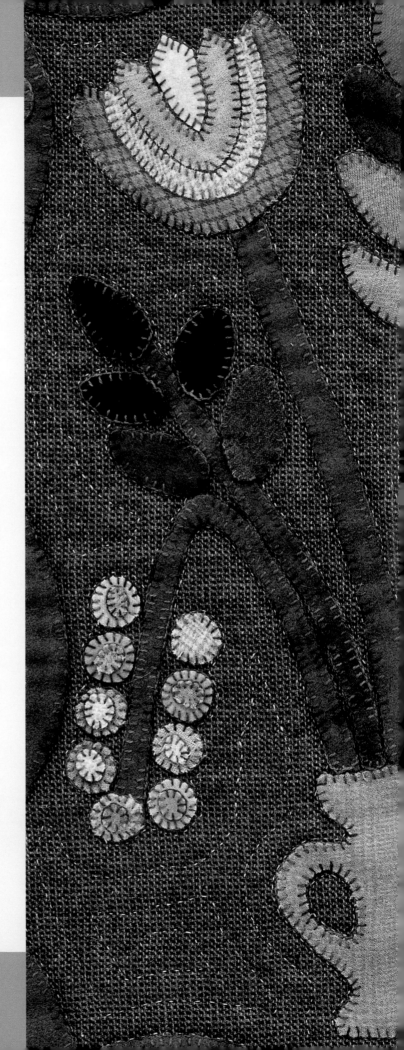

Hooked on Wool:
Rugs, Quilts, and More

© 2006 by Martingale & Company

Martingale®
& COMPANY

That Patchwork Place® is an imprint of
Martingale & Company®.

Martingale & Company
20205 144th Avenue NE
Woodinville, WA 98072-8478 USA
www.martingale-pub.com

Credits

President: Nancy J. Martin

CEO: Daniel J. Martin

VP and General Manager: Tom Wierzbicki

Publisher: Jane Hamada

Editorial Director: Mary V. Green

Managing Editor: Tina Cook

Developmental and
   Technical Editor: Karen Costello Soltys

Copy Editor: Sheila Chapman Ryan

Design Director: Stan Green

Illustrator: Laurel Strand

Cover and Text Designer: Stan Green

Photographer: Brent Kane

Thanks to Phil and Janet Reda of Woodinville, Washington, for allowing us to photograph the projects for this book in their lovely home.

Printed in China
11 10 09 08 07 06   8 7 6 5 4 3 2 1

Library of Congress Cataloging-in-Publication Data

Hooked on wool : rugs, quilts, and more / compiled and edited by Karen Costello Soltys.
        p. cm.
    ISBN 1-56477-656-5
1. Hooking. 2. Woolen goods. I. Soltys, Karen Costello.
    TT833.H66 2006
    746.7'4—dc22

                                    2005022844

Mission Statement

Dedicated to providing quality products and service to inspire creativity.

Contents

8

Welcome, Friends!

Part of the fun of being a how-to book editor is gaining exposure to the newest techniques, seeing wonderful designs as they arrive in our office, and especially having the opportunity to meet and work with some very talented people.

Compiling the set of exceptional projects you'll find in this book gave me the chance to renew old friendships with some of the designers, and to cultivate new ones with people whom I hadn't met but whose designs I admired. While I know you'll thoroughly enjoy browsing through the project photos and stitching or hooking or felting the projects in this book, I wanted you to know what a great group of people these designers are. In addition to their fun projects, you'll also learn from their tips that they are so willing to share.

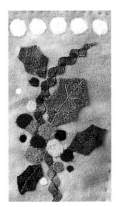

One of the newer techniques you'll discover in this book is the art of needle felting. If you haven't yet tried it, I encourage you to do so. Linda Lenich and Jennifer Zoeterman of Pure Wool have added pretty touches of colorful wool roving (or fleece as they call it) to their appliquéd Christmas projects. Their designs contain just enough felting to whet your appetite and prime you for your next felting project. These designers also have a clever way to make your own wool rickrack for embellishing an appliqué project.

Another fun part of this book is finding new uses for hooked rugs. For instance, Nola A. Heidbreder, a popular rug-hooking teacher, has created two wonderful hooked purses. They're easy to hook and finish by hand, and of course they're lined with wool. They're fun and funky and all your friends will want one.

Martingale & Company's own Donna Lever found another good way to display a hooked piece—as a lid topper for a wicker picnic basket (see facing page). Use the basket for your next family outing or for containing the wool for your next project—or simply make the topper to use as a table mat.

Of course there are more traditional hooked rugs and wool appliqué pieces, too. Try your hand at Polly Minick's unusual edge treatment of hooked lamb's tongues (shown above). Or follow Laurie Simpson's encouragement to cut your pieces free-form for her floral appliqué design. (Don't worry. We've provided patterns for the faint of heart!) Whichever project inspires you to "make me first," I'm sure that you'll come back again and again to the whimsical assortment of wool projects in *Hooked on Wool*.

Karen Costello Soltys

Editor

Working with Wool

All of the projects in this book are made predominantly of wool. So where do you find it and how do you make it ready to stitch or hook? Those are the questions that will be answered in this section.

New Wool, Old Wool

If you're lucky enough to live by a quilt shop or fabric store that carries new wool on the bolt, good for you! You already have a ready source of wool. If you don't have such a shop within driving distance, you can find new wool online or from many of the resources on page 91.

Another source is vintage wool. You have to be willing to spend a little time to search for wool garments, yardage, or blankets at thrift shops and yard sales, but sometimes you can find just the color you need for your project. It will require a bit of time to tear out the seams of garments, but if the color and texture are right, it can be worth your trouble.

With either new wool or old wool, the key is buying the right weight of wool, and washing and drying it to shrink slightly before beginning your project. Avoid gabardines and other slick or lightweight wools. Even after washing, they're just too limp to work with.

Instead, look for wool that has a little more substance to it. Blanket-weight wool is too heavy for rug hooking, but it can be perfect for the background of a penny rug. For appliqué shapes and rug-hooking strips, however, middleweight wool will work best. As an example, the kind of wool used to make a plaid skirt or men's wool shirt is perfect. And that goes for buying new wool off the bolt as well as for thrift shopping—it's only a bargain if you can use the wool in the end. Even if a skirt costs only two dollars, you've wasted two dollars if the wool is too wimpy and frays readily.

Preparing Wool

Whether you start with new wool right off the bolt, vintage wool, or a mix of old and new, the first thing you need to do is wash it. The fabric needs to shrink or felt slightly in order to give it the perfect texture for your project.

Wash the wool in your washing machine with a bit of detergent and hot water. Do not use fabric softener. Set the rinse cycle to cold. This change in temperature along with the agitation causes the wool to shrink. (If the wool you're starting with is already fairly heavy, you may want to wash and rinse it in warm water to prevent too much shrinking.) After the final rinse cycle, toss the wool in the dryer. Optimally, you'd like the wool to be damp upon removal; overdrying it in the dryer can create hard-to-remove wrinkles. You can lay it flat until it's completely dry, and then fold the wool yardage and store it to prevent unnecessary wrinkling.

If you are using vintage garments, after the initial washing you'll need to rip apart the seams, remove buttons, hems, plackets, and the like. Then it's a good idea to wash the wool again to get any dust and lint out of the seam areas and to close up the tiny holes made by the stitching. Dry as before, fold, and store.

Always wash used wool garments immediately upon bringing them home. You can wait until later to rip them apart and do the second washing, but you never know if you're inadvertently bringing in unwanted creatures, such as moths, on old wool clothing. If you find a bargain but don't have time to wash it, leave it in the trunk of your car until you're ready to launder it.

A Note about Overdyeing Wool

A few of the projects in this book use new wool right off the bolt. This is generally called "as-is" or "mill-dyed" wool. In some situations, as-is wool will give you just the look you want. Take a look at Pat Cross's Sheep's in the Meadow rug on page 78. She used almost exclusively as-is wool for this rug.

This wide variety of purple wools was used in Polka-Dot Chickens.

A sampling of as-is wools used for the Sheep's in the Meadow rug.

These days, more and more quilt and craft shops are carrying wools for penny rugs and hooked rugs, and you may be able to find both as-is and hand-dyed colors you like if you prefer to not dye your own wool.

Other times, you may want colors that are subtle or plaids that look a bit more blended than new wool. In that case, you can overdye the fabrics. A good example of this is Polly Minick's Polka-Dot Chickens rug on page 36. She used nine different purple wools that started out as various plaids, checks, and tweeds. To make all the fabrics blend together, all of the wools were overdyed in the same purple dye formula. Some-times these dyed wools are referred to as "textured" since the colors are blended, but you can still see the plaid, check, or tweed pattern which gives visual texture to the project. Other times a plain wool is overdyed, and the result is a wool with mottled color. You'll find quite a few books on dyeing wool, complete with instructions and dye recipes for a wide variety of colors. Ask at your local fabric shop or check online retailers for books on the subject.

An as-is plaid was the basis for Hearts versus Stars on page 64. Hand-dyed colors to complement the plaid round out the color scheme.

Wool Appliqué

If you're new to wool appliqué, making your first penny rug or wool quilt will be a treat. The whole process is fairly quick and easy. You don't need very many tools or supplies, and once your shapes are prepared, your project is quite portable. If you're familiar with traditional hand appliqué, you'll be surprised at how much easier it is to make and stitch wool shapes. There are no seam allowances to turn under. And the blanket stitch, which is traditionally used to hold the shapes in place, goes much quicker than traditional hand appliqué.

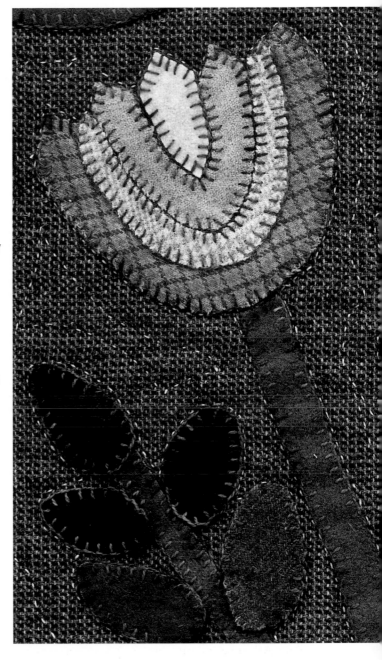

Tools and Supplies

Aside from to the wool you need, you may already have everything else you need for your project in your sewing room or kitchen.

Template Materials

The easiest way to make patterns for wool appliqué is to trace the pattern onto freezer paper and then use that pattern to cut out the wool shapes. You can find freezer paper at most grocery stores in the same aisle where the plastic wraps and aluminum foil are displayed.

If your pattern has a lot of repeat shapes in it, you may also want to have some template plastic on hand.

That way, you can trace the shape onto the template plastic and then use the template to make multiple copies of the pattern on freezer paper.

A black fine-point permanent marker is also a vital item. It's good for tracing patterns onto plastic, freezer paper, or fusible web. You'll want one or more of these in your sewing kit.

Scissors

Fabric shears are good for cutting out larger pieces, such as the background piece and any of the larger appliqués. You may find smaller scissors easier to control when cutting smaller detailed shapes. In addition, you'll need embroidery scissors or thread snips for hand-sewing purposes.

Needles and Threads

Look for larger hand-sewing needles, such as size 20 or 22 chenille needles. Tapestry needles work well, but make sure the point isn't too blunt to go through your wool. Also make sure that the eye of the needle is large enough to fit two strands of floss or a single strand of pearl cotton.

Everyone seems to have her own personal favorite when it comes to thread for wool appliqué. Embroidery floss comes in the largest variety of colors, so if you're looking for a perfect color match, floss may be for you. Floss is six-stranded thread, packaged in skeins. For wool appliqué, you need two strands at a time. Simply cut your thread to length and then peel off the strands you need.

Pearl cotton is a twisted thread and is also sold in skeins. It comes in various weights or thicknesses: size 3, 5, 8, and 12. Size 3 is the thickest; size 12 is the finest. For blanket-stitching, size 8 works well. If you're working on a large piece with chunky shapes, then you may be able to use size 5. Pearl cotton tends to add a little more dimension to your work than floss does because the thread is round rather than flat. However, it is available in fewer colors than floss.

Another option is to use wool floss or tapestry wool. Like pearl cotton, wool floss can add a nice dimension to your work, but work with short lengths because it can fray apart at the eye of the needle as you pull the needle in and out of the fabric. Laurie Simpson's wool quilt Taupe Garden on page 72 shows how variegated wool can enhance the look of an appliquéd project.

Basting Supplies

To hold the wool appliqués in place, you may either pin them or adhere them some other way. Using the pins you already own may be the best option for you. If you find that the pins are getting in the way and snag your thread, you may want to look for another option.

Some crafters prefer to use a spray adhesive on the back of their pieces. This allows you to stick the pieces in place where you want them without the use of pins. Another "sticky" option is to use a glue stick made especially for use on fabric. A daub of glue stick on the back of your appliqués should be enough to hold them in place until they are secured with stitching. Liquid fabric glue isn't a good option because it dries hard and will show up in your finished work by darkening the fabric.

STAPLE BASTING

For a really secure hold, and one that won't hamper your stitching, try stapling the appliqués in place. Staples don't have sharp tips sticking out to grab your thread, and they're really handy, especially if you plan to transport your project. You can be sure those pieces won't fall off! To remove the staples when you're through, simply lift them off with the type of staple remover that looks like a letter opener, rather than the spring-loaded claw type of remover.

Making Templates

Some shapes, such as vines or stripes, can be cut without templates. You can simply cut a straight strip of fabric and appliqué it in place. If the vine is to be gently curved, you can still use a strip of fabric cut on the straight of grain because the wool is flexible enough to bend somewhat. Other shapes will require templates, and you can trace the patterns from the book directly onto freezer paper if you like. If you'll need multiple pieces of a pattern, it's a good idea to make a plastic template first.

1. Trace the pattern onto the template plastic and cut out the shape on the drawn line.

2. Trace around the plastic template onto the dull (noncoated) side of the freezer paper as many times as needed. (While you can get away with reusing freezer-paper shapes for cotton appliqué, it's a good idea to make one template for each piece needed

when working with wool. When you peel the paper off of the wool, you'll see that quite a bit of fuzz sticks to the paper, making it hard to adhere it to the wool a second or third time.)

3. Cut out the freezer-paper shapes about ¼" outside of the drawn lines.

Preparing Appliqués

Getting your appliqué shapes ready for your project is quite easy. You can use either side of the wool, you don't need to allow extra fabric for a seam allowance, and you don't have to worry about grain line, either. You can cut shapes in any direction to make the best use of your fabric—if you want plaids or checks to run diagonally across the appliqué, cut them that way. If you want to take advantage of dark or light shading in a hand-dyed wool, place the templates accordingly.

1. Decide which side of the wool you want to use and then press the freezer-paper template, shiny side down, onto the right side of the wool.

2. Cut out each shape, cutting directly on the lines. Peel the paper off of the wool. (You may want to leave the paper patterns in place until you're ready to appliqué.)

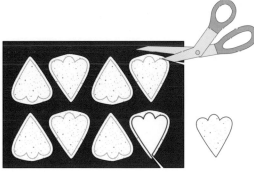

3. Secure the pieces to the background or on top of whatever other shape they will be appliquéd to.

Stitching Techniques

In simple patterns, a shape is appliquéd directly onto the background fabric. In some of the more complex designs, the appliqué shapes are layered, one on top of another. For these types of units, start stitching with the topmost piece and work your way to the bottom.

This way, you'll never be appliquéing through more than one underneath layer, and you'll always have a place to hide your starting and stopping knots.

Most of the appliqué projects in the book use blanket-stitch appliqué. However, some of the more primitive-looking projects use a whipstitch, which is a little less elaborate. Other stitch details are also used to embellish some of the projects. You'll find illustrations of those stitches below.

Blanket stitch

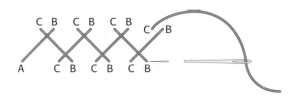

Herringbone stitch

Running stitch

Stem stitch

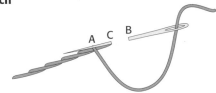

Whipstitch

Caring for Your Wool Projects

Projects stitched in wool need very little in the way of maintenance. You don't need to (and really shouldn't) press the completed rug. You don't want to flatten the wool or put sheen on it. If you fold it for storage, you may find that it needs a bit of pressing to get out a crease. Try steaming it from the wrong side, holding your iron above the fabric. If this isn't enough, you can place a damp towel on the wrong side of the penny rug and press.

Don't wash your penny rug either by hand or machine, and don't dry-clean it. If something gets spilled on it, use a damp cloth or sponge to mop up the liquid. You'll find that wool is very resilient and spills should bead up on the wool rather than soak right in. To remove dust or pet hair, you can shake out the rug or use a lint brush. The masking tape variety works well on stitched projects; take care when using them on needle-felted fleece.

Needle Felting

Needle felting is both fast and easy to do, and offers you a new way to add color and texture to your wool projects. Using a barbed felting needle, you push colored wool fleece, or roving, into the wool background fabric. Pushing the needle in and out of the fleece and background causes the barb on the needle to entangle the wool fibers of the fleece with the wool background fabric, and makes the fleece stays in place. You can make any shape you want from the fleece, from leaves and flower petals to round berries and long, twining vines.

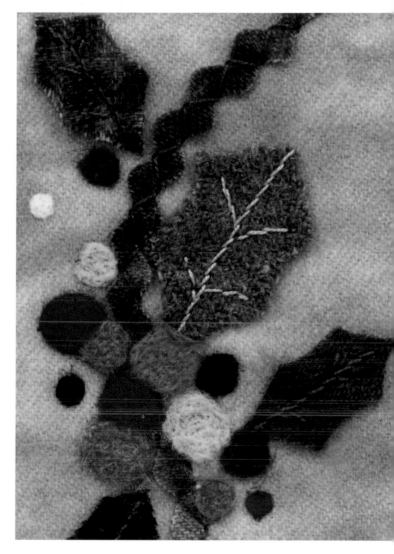

Needle felting adds a whole new dimension to wool appliqué projects. The fibers are held in place without stitching.

Tools and Supplies

You'll need just a few supplies in addition to the rest of your wool-appliqué materials. If your local quilt shop or craft store doesn't carry roving/fleece and felting needles, see "Resources" on page 91 for supplies. Foam can generally be found at fabric and craft stores.

- **Felting needle.** This barbed tool is very sharp and the tip is fragile, so handle it with care. Always store it safely away to prevent an accident.

- **Dense foam.** A 6" to 12" square of foam makes a great work surface. Foam needs to be 2" to 3" thick.

- **Fleece or roving.** Pick a selection of colors to complement your project. Fleece, which is also called *roving*, is often sold in packages of several colors or shades of a color together. The roving is generally rolled into a loose ball. Unroll a section and pull off as much as you'll need for your motif. You can purchase dyed fleece in a wide variety of solid and variegated colors.

How to Needle Felt

1. Place the foam on your work surface to protect it and the tip of the needle as you work.

2. Lay the wool background fabric on top of the foam, right side up.

3. Unroll a section of fleece, and then gently pull a small amount from one end. Wool fleece goes a long way, so don't pull off too much—you can always add more if needed. Do not use scissors to cut the fleece; the blunt end of the cut fleece will interfere with the felting process.

4. Place the fleece in the desired position on the wool background. Hold the needle between your thumb and index finger, around the center of the shaft. Make sure to hold the needle upright (perpendicular to your work, not slanted), and push the needle through the fleece into the wool background and down into the foam work surface. Use a firm but gentle up-and-down motion, always keeping your hand away from the needle tip.

5. Continue needling the fleece into position by bringing the needle up and down in a sewing-machine fashion. Once the center of the shape is held in place, use the tip of the needle to move the fibers into the desired shape, such as a leaf or stem.

REARRANGING FLEECE

It's easy to make a change to your needle-felted design, as long as you felt the shapes lightly to start. By making just a few pokes with the needle to hold each shape in place, you can review your work and decide if you like your color arrangement and the position of each motif. If you want to change something, simply pull the fleece off of the background fabric and reuse it at another spot, or save it for another project. It's totally reusable.

The more you needle your fleece, the more compact and interlocked with the background fabric it will become. You can needle very close together around the edges for a secure hold and leave the center of a motif less felted for a loftier look. Or you can needle the entire motif heavily for a more compact look. Turn your work over and look at the underside to see how the fleece fibers have been pushed through the wool.

You can needle felt at an angle, but be careful to keep your hand out of the way and to not bend the needle. It is slim and fragile, so don't press too hard while needling.

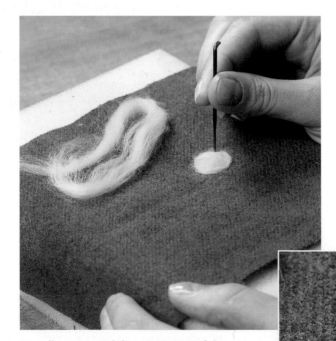

Needling around the perimeter of the shape will hold the edges neatly in place. You can needle as much or as little as you like in the center; heavy needling will make a flatter shape.

Rug Hooking

Like wool appliqué, rug hooking is a fun fiber-art form that is easy to learn. Before you can start hooking, you'll need to transfer your pattern or design onto your desired rug backing fabric and cut the wool you plan to use into strips. This section covers basic supplies and instructions.

Tools and Supplies

If you have a quilting hoop and a rotary cutter, all you need is a rug hook, a piece of rug-backing fabric, and wool, and you can get started. Of course, like any craft, there are lots of tools available to make the process more enjoyable. So let's take a closer look at the variety of tools and supplies available to rug hookers.

Backing Fabrics

Most rugs are hooked into one of three types of fabric: Scottish burlap, monk's cloth, or linen. What these fabrics have in common is a regular, open weave that allows you to fit a hook through the fabric and stay on the grain. Scottish burlap is the least expensive choice, but it is also the roughest of the three fabrics. Monk's cloth is a much softer, flexible fabric. You might find it in craft shops in a large open weave for afghan making, but be sure to purchase the variety with the smaller openings for rug hooking. Finally, there is linen. This is the most expensive option, and it is soft to the touch and is easy to hook through. Many rug hookers start out working with burlap because it's readily available, and is most often used in beginner kits. If you find burlap to be too scratchy, you may want to opt for either monk's cloth or linen. If you can't find these fabrics at your local quilt or fabric shop, you can buy them via the Internet. See "Resources" on page 91.

Transfer Supplies

You'll need to transfer your desired pattern onto the backing fabric. Complete instructions for doing that are given in "Transfer the Pattern" on page 22. Here, we'll just review the supplies you need for this task.

- **Full-sized pattern.** Most of the patterns in the book have been reduced to fit onto a book page. You'll need to enlarge the pattern to full size, either with a photocopier that makes enlargements or by hand. If enlarging by hand, you'll need paper large enough to fit the complete design.

- **Red Dot Tracer or craft netting.** To transfer the design onto the backing fabric, you'll need to make a copy of the pattern that you can trace over to transfer the ink onto the rug-backing fabric. Red Dot Tracer is similar to nonwoven interfacing, and has red dots marked at 1" intervals. It's permeable, so when you trace over it with a permanent marker, the ink will seep through onto the backing fabric. Likewise, craft netting or tulle has an open weave that lets you see through to the original pattern and allows the ink to flow through the openings to mark the backing fabric. Either of these options can be found in fabric stores and are quite inexpensive.

- **Indelible fine-point marker.** This is needed to transfer the design onto the backing fabric. Make sure the marker is permanent so that once the ink is dry it won't rub off onto your wool or hands as you hook.

- **Masking tape.** You'll need to tape the backing fabric and pattern in place to prevent shifting as you transfer the design.

Hooks

If you've ever bought a rug-hooking kit, chances are it came with a rug hook. These hooks are inexpensive and do the trick. At some point you may want to upgrade to a different-style handle, or even a different-shape hook. So many choices are available to you! Short, rounded ball handles; long, pencil-type handles; and mid-sized ergonomic handles each have their fans. If you have a shop nearby where you can try them out, you're in luck. If not, you can find all sorts of hooks available on the Internet. Prices range from about $5 to $30, depending on the type of wood used for the handle and the style of the hook.

Most of the projects in this book use wide cuts of wool, so a primitive hook with a medium shaft will work well. Hooks for traditional rug hooking have much finer shafts that can't handle wider cuts of wool.

Hoops and Frames

It's important that your backing fabric be held taut when you are rug hooking so that you can make consistent-sized loops and achieve uniform coverage. You can put your fabric either in a quilting hoop or on a rug-hooking frame. If you already own a quilting hoop, you might want to start with that. A 14" hoop works well, because you can fit a fairly large hooking area inside the hoop, yet it isn't so large as to be unwieldy. You can also use a hoop on a tabletop or floor stand if you have one. One nice

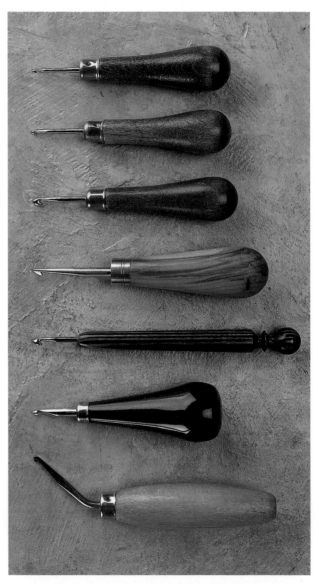

Rug hooks come in a variety of handle shapes and hook contours, making selecting one a very personal choice.

Puritan frame with gripper strips

Bliss table-top cutter

Gruber quilting frame with swivel base

Townsend clamp-style cutter

benefit of working in a hoop is that you can rotate it easily as needed to change your hooking direction. If your hoop on a stand swivels, you'll find that to be a practical feature.

Unlike round quilting hoops, rug-hooking frames are generally rectangular. Many styles are available, but they all have needle-gripper strips to hold your work securely. Prices vary widely on frames, depending on whether they swivel, tilt, collapse for storage, or have tightening ratchets. The choice of frame or hoop is strictly personal, so it's a good idea to try out various types before buying.

Strip Cutter or Rotary Cutter

The final item you'll need for rug hooking is a tool for cutting wool strips. Today, most rug hookers cut their strips with a strip cutter. These gadgets let you cut two or more strips at a time by cranking a handle to feed wool through the blades. They make quick work of cutting strips on grain, but they require an investment ranging from about $140 to $400. Rest assured, you do not need a strip cutter to make a hooked rug, although they are very handy. You can use a rotary cutter, mat, and ruler used for quiltmaking, which you probably already own.

Getting Started

The first thing you need to do is prepare your backing fabric. You'll need to transfer the design to your backing fabric and finish the edges of the fabric to prevent fraying while you're hooking. You'll also need to decide how you want to finish the edges of your completed rug because some methods require up-front preparation. For more details, see "Finishing Your Rug" on page 26.

Prepare the Backing Fabric

First, determine how big your project design area is. Then add about 8" to each dimension if you'll be hooking on a frame or 16" if you'll be hooking in a hoop. Cut your backing fabric to your calculated size. For instance, if your finished rug will be 12" x 18", cut your backing fabric 20" x 26" for hooking on a frame, or 28" x 34" for hooking in a hoop.

After cutting your backing fabric to size, you'll need to finish the edges so they won't fray. (No matter which type of backing fabric you use, the edges will fray easily.) If you have a serger, you can quickly and easily serge the edges. Another option is to zigzag stitch them on your regular sewing machine. If neither of these ideas appeal to you, you can fold a strip of masking tape over each edge, encasing the loose fibers.

If you don't have lots of excess backing fabric or you don't want to spend a lot of money on fabric that will later be cut away, you can get away with a smaller piece of backing fabric. You'll still need to leave a few inches beyond your finished rug dimensions, but then you can add on extensions of scrap fabric to make your backing large enough to fit into your hoop. You can machine stitch strips of cotton, flannel, or wool to the edges of your rug backing to make it the full 8" or 16" larger than the design area. Adding extension strips to your backing fabric eliminates the need to finish the backing edges with tape or by serging them. When you're through with your project, you can remove the strips and save them to reuse on your next rug. Thrifty!

Transfer the Pattern

Most rug-hooking patterns are sold as a design already transferred to the backing fabric. Some designers offer you a choice of background fabric (linen, burlap, or monk's cloth). To use the patterns in this book, or to create your own patterns, you'll need to transfer the design onto the backing fabric yourself. It's not hard to do, and it's a good skill to know because then you'll have the flexibility of making printed patterns any size you want and the freedom to design your own rugs. Transferring the pattern requires just a few steps.

1. Enlarge the pattern to the desired size. The patterns in this book all list the percentages you'll need to enlarge them to make rugs the same size as the ones pictured. You can enlarge them yourself on a photocopier, take them to a copy shop and have them enlarged for you (a good option for patterns that need to be enlarged more than 200%), or enlarge them by hand, following the grid printed behind each pattern.

2. Tape the full-sized paper pattern to a large flat surface such as a table or floor (wood or vinyl; not carpeted). Lay Red Dot Tracer or craft netting over the pattern, smooth it out, and tape it in place.

3. Using a permanent fine-point marker, trace over every line in the printed pattern. You can use a ruler to help guide you along straight lines, such as borders, if desired. Lift the Red Dot Tracer or netting from the pattern and check to make sure that all lines have been copied.

4. Lay your prepared backing fabric onto the same large flat surface. Make sure the grain lines are straight and that there are no creases or wrinkles in the fabric, and then tape it in place. Lay the Red Dot Tracer or netting pattern over the backing fabric, centering the pattern over the fabric and making sure that the outer edges of the design are aligned with the straight grain of the fabric. If you don't align the pattern with the fabric grain, your rug will tend to twist out of shape as you work on it. Tape the pattern in place securely.

5. Using a permanent marker, trace over the Red Dot Tracer or netting pattern again. This time, the tracings will go through the pattern to mark the design onto the backing fabric. Before removing the pattern completely, lift up one corner and check the backing fabric to make sure that all parts of the

design have been marked. Fill in any missing lines and then remove the pattern from the backing fabric.

Decide on a Finishing Technique

Some of the techniques used to finish the edges of a hooked rug are easier to do if you start them before you begin to hook. If you want to use rug-binding tape, for instance, it's quicker and easier if you sew it by machine to the rug backing before there are hooked loops in the way. Other techniques can be started and completed after all hooking is complete. See "Finish Your Rug" for more details on finishing options.

Cut the Strips

Once you've decided on your color scheme and gathered your wool, you'll need to cut your wool into strips. You'll need wool that's about four to six times larger than the area to be covered, so plan accordingly. You don't need to cut all your strips at once, and perhaps it's better if you don't. They can tend to get tangled, and if you don't use all the strips, it's hard to determine how much wool you have in square inches once it's cut. (This is okay if you like to make scrappy rugs, but if you're trying to determine if you have enough of your leftover strips to fill a specific area on another rug, it can be a little tricky.) If you plan to use a mix of wools, such as three or four different reds, cut a few strips from each wool so you can mix up the strips as you hook.

Each project in the book tells you what size to cut the strips. Most are size 8, but some do use narrower strips, so be sure to read the directions before you cut anything. In rug hooking, strips are given as number sizes, size 3 through size 9 or 10. These sizes indicate the number of $1/32$" in each strip width. For instance, size 8 is $8/32$", or $1/4$" wide. Size 6 is $6/32$", or $3/16$" wide. If you use a strip cutter, you simply attach the size blade required and your strips will be cut uniformly to that size. If you use a rotary cutter, you'll find it's easier to cut $1/4$"-wide strips than it is to do narrower ones. If you need size 6 strips, you can start by cutting strips $3/8$" wide, then snipping one end of the strip in the center and tearing it into two narrower strips.

STAY ON GRAIN

Make sure to always cut the wool strips on grain. Because the strips are narrow, if they are cut slightly off grain, they will tend to fray or tear apart as you pull them through the backing fabric. To make sure you're working on grain, make a snip at one end of the wool and then tear a narrow piece of wool away from the main piece. Wool will always tear on the grain, so now you know you have a perfectly straight edge that is on grain.

The Hooking Technique

The basic hooking technique is easy to master. First, we'll review how to hook, followed by pointers for the best order in which to hook and how to change direction.

Starting and Stopping

To begin, put your backing fabric into your hoop or onto your frame. It needs to be completely taut and not skewed—the weave of the fabric should look nice and square. Hold your hook in your dominant hand as you would hold a knife, and hold a strip between the thumb and forefinger of your other hand. (Our diagrams show right-handed hooking, but you can just as easily hook left-handed.)

1. Push the tip of the hook through a hole in the backing fabric, hook it around the wool strip, and pull up the short end so that a wool tail of about $1/2$" to 1" shows above the backing fabric. If you've pulled up more than this, simply tug on the strip from beneath the backing fabric to adjust the tail length.

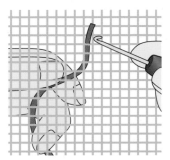

2. Holding the strip with one hand from beneath the backing fabric, poke the hook with your other hand through the next hole in the backing fabric and pull up a loop. The loops should be roughly the same height as the width of the strip. It is often easier to pull the loop up a little higher than necessary, then gently pull from underneath until the loop is at the desired height.

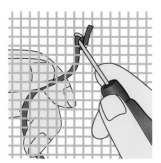

3. Continue hooking loops in this manner, following the grid of the backing fabric. Depending on how wide your strips are you will need to skip a hole between each loop or after every second or third loop. The goal is to have the loops touch one another so that you can't see through to the backing fabric, but not have them packed so tightly together that they are crushing one another. It's common for beginners to hook the loops too close together, which makes it hard for the finished rug to lie flat.

4. When you reach the end of a strip or you need to end the color you're working with, pull the tail up through the top of the fabric. Again, leave about ½" to 1" and clip off the rest of the strip. The tails will be clipped off later, even with the height of the loops. To start a new strip, pull up the tail as before, this time pulling it up through the same hole as your ending tail. Continue hooking.

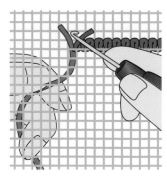

5. When the area around the beginning and ending tails has been hooked, you can trim the tails so that they are even with the surrounding loops. Hold your scissors parallel to the rug surface with the blades even with the loops. Snip the tails off and notice how well the tail ends blend with the loops.

Even though you start a new strip in the same hole where you just ended, it's not a good idea to have too many tails in the same area. The starting and stopping tails fill in a space as well as a loop, but they aren't rounded on the top. If you have places in your rug where the starting and stopping points line up side by side from one row to the next, these spots will be noticeable in the finished rug.

If you find that you're running out of a strip and it's bound to end right next to where you ended in the previous row of hooking, simply stop hooking that strip sooner, snip off the excess length, and start up with a new strip. Your rug will look more professional.

Hooking Direction

Now that you've practiced hooking in a straight line, it's time to make things a little more interesting. Depending on the pattern you choose, you may need to hook in circles, swirls, or in different directions.

It is possible to learn to hook in any direction, although hooking toward yourself is usually the most comfortable position. No matter what direction you're hooking, the goal is to keep the wool strip on the underside of the rug flat and untwisted. By turning the angle of your hook slightly, you can make loops that start to turn a corner. If you find this hard to do, you can simply turn your hoop slightly so that you're still hooking toward yourself. If you're working on a frame, you can turn the frame, or simply lift your work from the gripper strips and reposition it. This way you can hook completely around a circle or make gentle curves.

If you need to turn a corner, however, you may want to end the strip and start with a new one working in the new direction. You don't want to twist the strip underneath the rug, or carry the strip over other parts that have already been hooked. This will put more wear and tear on the strips and shorten the life of your rug. However, one place you don't want to start and stop is at the corner of a border, where snipped-off tails will be more noticeable. It's best if you can hook along one edge of the border and turn the corner using the same strip. Then start a new strip somewhere along the straightaway.

Swirls in the sheep can suggest a curly fleece.

Hooking Order

It's a good idea to come up with a plan for what to hook first and what to save for last. The projects in this book all specify a logical hooking sequence, but there are some basic rules to follow for any pattern you decide to hook.

1. If there are any grid lines in your rug, such as in the Hit-or-Miss Footstool on page 82, hook these first.

2. Hook the row that separates the border from the interior of the rug. Taking care of these lines now assures that they will be hooked on grain and that you won't have to make room to squeeze them in later.

3. Hook motifs starting in the center of the rug and work outward. For primitive-style hooking, shapes are often outlined first (in matching or contrasting wool) and then filled in. Hook the outline just inside the drawn line or your shapes will turn out too large.

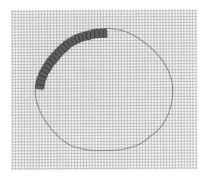

Hook inside the drawn lines.

4. Hook the border next to make sure that it is worked on grain.

5. Fill in the background last. If desired, you could hook a row or two around the motifs as you're working on the rug to make sure you are satisfied with your background color choices. However, it's a good idea to complete the border before filling in the background area completely. Depending on the look you want, you can hook the background back and forth in rows, you can follow the outlines of the motifs, or you can even add swirling lines in large open parts of the background for additional interest.

Finishing Your Rug

Many of the projects in this book are finished in different fashions: some have rug-binding tape, some have edges whipstitched with wool yarn, and there's even one that is finished with a fabric facing. When it comes to making any of the rugs in this book, you can select the method you like best. You don't need to finish your rug in the same manner as shown on the original project.

Blocking

It's fairly common for a finished rug to not be completely square or lie flat. Sometimes, from pulling it taut in the hoop or frame, it becomes a little bit misshapen. That's where blocking comes in.

To block your rug, tug on the backing fabric to pull it back into shape. Then lay the rug right side down on your ironing board or other firm, flat surface. Cover it with a damp towel, and then press it with an iron set on steam. Do not iron back and forth, but rather stamp the iron up and down, using firm pressure. Press the entire piece, and then turn the rug over and repeat the stamping process. The steam will help reshape the wool and give a smooth appearance to your finished rug, hiding any uneven loops. Remove the towel and allow the rug to dry flat overnight or until it's completely dry.

Rug-Binding Tape

One common method for finishing a rug is to attach purchased twill tape to the outer perimeter of the design. When the rug is completed, the tape is folded to the wrong side of the rug and whipstitched in place. If desired, you can preshrink the tape by soaking it in warm water and allowing it to dry before using. This will prevent any potential shrinking or color bleeding during the steam blocking process. However, since you won't be laundering or dry-cleaning your rug, this step isn't essential.

Purchase enough rug-binding tape to go completely around the perimeter of your design, plus a few extra inches for turning the corners and for overlapping at the ends. If you want to attach the tape by machine, it's best to do this prior to hooking your rug so that you can stitch it right up to the edge of the design.

Once you've hooked loops, it will be impossible to machine stitch closely to the edge because of the bulk of the loops. Of course you can still choose this option for rugs that have already been hooked. You'll simply need to sew the binding tape to the rug by hand.

1. On your rug backing, draw a line ⅛" outside of the border, using a ruler if your rug has straight edges. (You may need to "eyeball" curved edges.)

2. Lay the binding tape on top of the backing fabric so that the tape overlaps the design area and the edge is aligned with the drawn line. Pin in place. Fold about 1" of the starting end back under itself so that the raw edge won't show once the binding is complete.

3. Stitch the tape in place, stitching ⅛" from the edge of the tape and overlapping the ends of the tape. When you come to a corner, you will need to pleat the tape so that you can turn the corner later. This pleat will give you enough ease to turn the tape to the back side of the rug when hooking is complete.

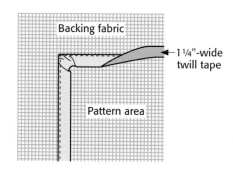

4. Fold the tape back, away from the design area, and baste it in place to hold it out of your way.

5. After all hooking is complete, trim the excess backing fabric, leaving about 1" of backing that will be covered with the twill tape. Cut the corners at an angle to reduce bulk. Then fold the tape and the excess backing to the wrong side of the rug. Fold a miter at each corner and pin in place. Whipstitch the edge of the tape in place on the back of the rug,

taking care to sew only through the backing fabric and not through the wool loops.

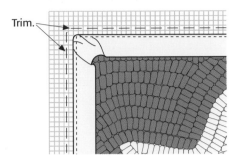

Trim.

Whipstitching with Yarn

A popular finish for primitive rugs is to whipstitch the edges with wool yarn that matches or coordinates with your rug border. This can be done as a flat finish as described below, or filled with cording to round the edges, as explained in "Whipstitching over Cording" at right. You will need 100%-wool yarn, such as three-ply tapestry yarn, or worsted-weight knitting yarn, and a large-eye needle.

1. Mark a line 1" away from the last row of hooking on all sides of the rug.

2. Zigzag stitch along the marked lines and then trim the excess backing fabric to just outside of the zigzag stitching.

3. Fold the rug-backing fabric toward the front of the rug so the raw edge just meets the last row of loops. Fold again in the same manner, so you have a folded edge that is approximately ¼" to ⅜" wide. At the corners, trim some of the excess fabric off at an angle to reduce bulk. Then fold the fabric toward the right side of the rug, folding each side of the corners toward one another to form a miter. If desired, you can use quilting thread to baste the folds in place so that you won't have to hold them as you whipstitch with yarn.

4. Thread a tapestry needle with two or three plies of tapestry yarn or one strand of worsted-weight knitting yarn, about 18" to 24" long. Whipstitch the yarn around the folded edge of backing fabric. To start, bring the needle up from the back of the

rug, right at the edge of the loops. Leave a 2" tail of yarn. Then simply wrap the yarn around the folded edge and stick the needle up through the back of the rug, right next to the first stitch. As you continue to make stitches, make sure they cover the yarn tail. Continue sewing in this manner, whipstitching the wool around the binding until the entire fold of backing fabric has been covered.

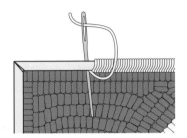

5. To end each length of yarn, simply slide the needle back through the stitches you've already taken (on the back of the rug) for about 1". Bring the needle up and snip off the excess yarn.

Whipstitching over Cording

This finishing method is similar to whipstitching without cording, although it does require the extra step of also adding twill tape. It makes a nice firm edge around the rug, which will be about the same height as the hooked loops. The finish is durable, and thus a good choice for rugs that will be used on the floor.

For this method, you will need 100%-wool yarn and a large-eye tapestry needle for whipstitching, quilting thread for sewing, ¼"-diameter cotton cording (used for corded edges in pillows and upholstery), and twill rug-binding tape. Allow enough tape and cording to go around the perimeter of your rug, plus some extra for shrinking and overlapping. If you are concerned about shrinking during blocking, you can soak both the tape and cording in warm water and allow to air-dry before using them.

1. Mark a line 1¼" outside of the last row of hooking on all sides of the rug.

2. Zigzag stitch along the marked lines and then trim the excess backing fabric away, just outside of the zigzag stitching.

3. Lay your project face down on the table and place the preshrunk cotton cording along the outside edge of your hooking. Roll the edge of backing fabric over the cording (toward the back of the rug) and pin it in place all around the perimeter of the rug.

4. Turn the rug so it is right side up. You should see a small width of the background fabric wrapped neatly over the cording around the entire project, just as piping goes around a pillow. Using quilting thread, hand baste through both layers of the un-hooked rug-backing fabric to encase the cording. Remove the pins as you go. Be careful not to catch the wool loops as you baste.

5. Thread a tapestry needle with three plies of wool yarn, about 18" to 24" long. Insert the needle through the back of the project through both layers of backing fabric. Leave a 2" tail of yarn on the back side of the project.

6. Working from left to right, bring the wool yarn up and over the cording and enter the needle directly next to the original starting point on the back. As you stitch, make sure that you hide the yarn tail with the whipstitches. Continue stitching in this manner until you are nearing the end of your yarn strand. Bring the yarn to the back of the rug and weave the needle under the whipstitches to hide the ending tail of yarn. Snip off any excess. Begin again with a new strand, hiding the tails and whip-stitching as before.

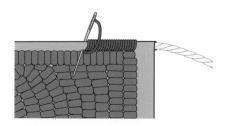

7. For a smooth finished edge, you'll need to stitch in each hole in the backing fabric so that the entire corded edge is covered and the backing fabric doesn't show through. When whipstitching over the corners of your rug, however, stitching once in each hole may not be enough for adequate cover-age. Try doubling up and taking two whipstitches

per hole as you turn the corner for a nicely rounded corner that is covered completely.

8. When all edges have been covered with yarn, add twill tape to the back of the rug to cover the raw edges of the backing fabric. Sew one edge of the twill tape as close to the whipstitched edges as possible. Use quilting thread that matches the color of your twill tape and stitch by hand. Pleat the corners to allow enough tape to miter them when you sew the opposite edge.

Edges are finished with yarn-covered cording, and excess backing fabric is hidden beneath twill tape.

9. If the raw edge of the backing fabric extends beyond the unsewn edge of the twill tape, trim the fabric as needed. Then hand stitch the remaining edge of the twill tape in place, mitering the corners as you go.

Caring for Your Hooked Rug

Because they're made of wool, hooked rugs are quite durable and resilient. Do not wash or dry-clean them. To maintain their beauty and their durability, periodically shake out the dust and sweep them with an electric broom or handheld sweeper; never use a vacuum cleaner with beater bars on your rug.

If a spill occurs, dab it up with a damp cloth. Most liquid spills will bead up on the wool, giving you time to blot them. If necessary, dampen a sponge or cloth and use a gentle soap sparingly to wipe away the spill. And, just as for appliquéd wool pieces, a masking-tape lint brush does wonders on hooked rugs when it comes to pet hair.

Basic Crochet

The Impressionistic Diamonds hooked purse on page 54 has crocheted granny square sides. If you know how to crochet, these squares will be quick and easy to make—follow the instructions starting on page 55. If you've never crocheted before, give it a try. The motion is very similar to that of rug hooking, and all that you need to know are a few basic stitches, which are illustrated here.

Holding the Hook

You can hold a crochet hook in one of two ways: like you'd hold a pencil, or like you'd hold your rug hook or a knife.

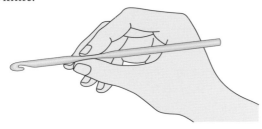

Hold hook like a pencil.

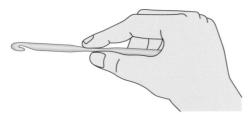

Hold hook like a knife or rug hook.

Start with a Slipknot

In order to make stitches, you first need to secure the yarn on your crochet hook. A basic slipknot is all that's needed. Make a loop near the end of the yarn by looping the tail up and over the yarn that's feeding off the ball or skein. Then reach into the loop, grasp the strand inside it, and pull the strand through the loop.

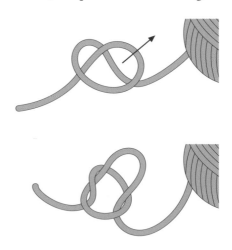

Place the loop on your crochet hook and pull the yarn tail until the knot is snug on the hook. Make sure it isn't too tight; the knot should be loose enough to easily slide along the hook.

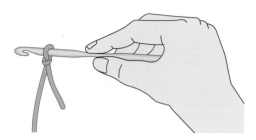

Making a Chain

Chain stitches are used to make a base chain—the starting point for your crochet. They are also used to create open spaces in granny squares.

1. Holding the slipknot between your thumb and forefinger of your nondominant hand and the yarn slightly taut in this same hand, wrap the yarn over the hook from right to left as shown below.

2. Pull the hook and the wrapped yarn through the slipknot until the knot comes off the hook. Note: Wrapping the yarn around your fingers as shown will help you keep even tension on the yarn as you crochet.

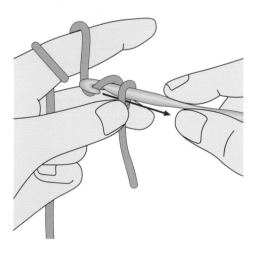

3. Continue making chain stitches in this manner until you have the total number required in the pattern instructions.

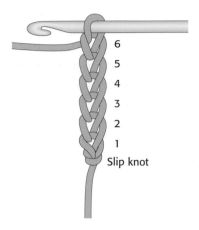

4. To join the chain to work in the round (which is how you'll be making a granny square), insert the crochet hook into the first chain stitch, wrap the yarn over the hook as before, and pull the yarn through both chain stitches on the hook. You now have a joined circle.

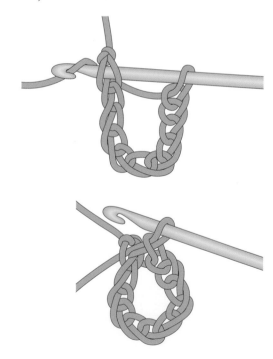

Double Crochet

This commonly used stitch involves multiple yarn wraps. At the start of the row or round, it is often used with a series of "turning chains," which is merely a specified number of chain stitches. Double crochets are generally made into a completed stitch, such as a chain stitch on the base chain or into the stitches of the previous row of crochet. For granny squares, the double crochets will be made into the open space of the starting ring, and then into the open spaces created by chain stitches as the pattern progresses.

1. Wrap the yarn over the hook. Insert the hook into the next stitch (or open space).

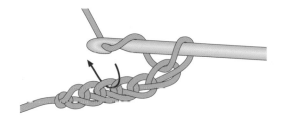

2. Wrap the yarn over the hook again and pull the yarn through the stitch or open space to the front of the work. Wrap the yarn over the hook again and pull it through two of the loops on the hook.

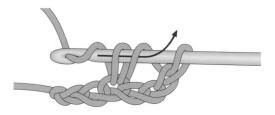

3. Wrap the yarn over the hook and pull it through the remaining two loops on the hook. One double crochet is now complete.

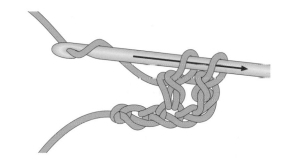

Rest Your Wings

Hooked Neckroll Pillow *by Bonnie Smith*

This charming angel pillow looks lovely atop a bed or settee, where the angel will welcome you or your guests to relax. Using the same plaid wool for hooking the background and assembling the pillow makes for a softly blended look.

Finished size of hooking: 17" x 14"
Finished pillow size: 6" diameter; 20" long

Materials

Wool yardage is based on 60"-wide wool (before washing). Amounts allow for four times the area to be hooked. Please allow extra wool if you hook high loops or tend to pack your loops close together. This pillow was hooked with size 7 strips.

- 1¼ yards of oatmeal-and-teal plaid wool for the hooked background and pillow

- 6" x 60" piece of mottled cream wool for the top of wings, face, and middle of heart

- 4" x 60" piece of textured or mottled aqua wool for the top of diamonds, outer edges of wings, and bottom of heart

- 4" x 60" piece of textured or mottled teal wool for the bottom of diamonds, stripe on wings, center of heart, and eyes

- 4" x 60" piece of textured or mottled oatmeal wool for the bottom of wings and top of heart

- 6" x 30" piece of mottled gold wool for the hair

- Scrap of rose wool for the mouth

- 22" x 25" piece of rug-backing fabric (30" x 33" if using a hoop)

- 30" of coordinating wool yarn or trim

- Red Dot Tracer

- Black permanent marker

- Bolster/pillow insert (6" x 20")

- Tapestry needle and heavy-duty thread

- Hand-sewing needle and thread to match background fabric

Cutting

The hooked piece shown was made using size 7 strips. Cut your wool into size 7 or 8 strips, but first cut or tear the plaid pieces needed to make the pillow covering. Cutting for the pillow pieces is based on a 6" x 20" pillow form. If your pillow form is different size, adjust the cut sizes accordingly. The cut sizes include seam allowances and extra for overlapping. You may want to cut the strips as you go so that you won't risk having your narrow strips tangle together.

From the oatmeal-and-teal plaid wool, cut or tear:
2 pieces, 5" x 19"
2 pieces, 7" x 24"

Hooking the Angel

1. Enlarge the pattern on page 35 as indicated. Then transfer the pattern onto your rug-backing fabric. For details on transferring patterns, see page 22. To make sure that the angel is transferred on the straight of grain, first draw a 14" x 17" rectangle centered on the backing fabric, following the grain of the fabric. These lines are the outer perimeter of the hooked area. Then trace the angel onto the fabric, centering her in the rectangle.

2. Hook the hair with gold wool, outlining it first and then filling in with gold.

3. Hook the eyes and mouth with teal and rose wool; then fill in the rest of the face with cream wool.

4. Hook the row of split diamonds below the face using aqua wool on the top of the diamonds and teal wool on the bottom. Hook the partial diamonds on each side of the face using oatmeal wool.

5. Hook the stripes on the wings using teal wool; then hook the area above and below the stripes with cream wool. Hook the outer edges of the wings with aqua wool, and complete the bottom of the wings with oatmeal wool.

6. The heart below the wings is hooked using the same color scheme as the wings: oatmeal, cream, aqua, and teal. Hook the small center portion with teal first and then work your way outward.

7. Outline the background area with the plaid wool and then outline the angel and heart. Finally, fill in all background areas with the plaid wool.

8. Block the pillow top, referring to page 26 for instructions. Let it dry flat.

Assembling the Pillow

1. Trim away the excess backing fabric, leaving approximately 1" around all edges. To prevent fraying, you can zigzag stitch or serge the edges with a sewing machine.

2. Sew a 5" x 19" piece of plaid wool to the top edge of the hooked pillow top. Both the wool and hooking are right side up, with wool overlapping the rug backing fabric. First match the midpoints of the hooked piece and wool strip and pin in place. Continue to pin the wool in place as close as possible to the last row of hooking. Using a hand-sewing needle and matching thread, sew the wool to the backing fabric with small stitches. The ends of the wool will extend beyond the edge of the hooking. Trim them even with the backing fabric. Repeat with the other 5" x 19" wool strip on the bottom edge of the hooked piece.

3. Sew the 7" x 24" wool pieces to the sides of the hooked piece in the same manner. Trim the excess wool at each end of the pillow even with the top and bottom wool pieces.

4. Roll the finished pillow top around the pillow insert, making sure it is centered from side to side. Overlap the long edges, folding under the raw edge of the piece that is laying on top, and pin in place to secure. (If you have too much overlap, you can tear some of the excess fabric away.) Then stitch the long edge in place by hand, using a small stitch and matching thread.

5. Gently gather the ends of the pillow to determine where to run the gathering stitches. Using heavy-duty thread and a tapestry needle, make long stitches at the point where you want to gather one end of the pillow. Pull the thread to gather and then tie the thread around the gather and knot to secure. Repeat on the opposite end.

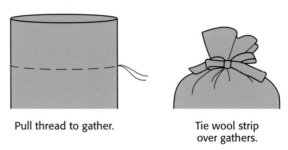

Pull thread to gather.

Tie wool strip over gathers.

6. Tear a ½"-wide strip of plaid wool. From this strip, cut two lengths, each approximately 15". Tie one strip around each gather to cover the stitching. If desired, you can fray the raw edges at each gathered end of the pillow. Simply pull off a couple of rows of thread to give your pillow a soft touch.

7. Cut two pieces of matching yarn or trim, each long enough to go around the circumference of the pillow. Lay the yarn or trim around the pillow at each end where the hooked work is stitched to the wool. Using matching thread, whipstitch over the yarn or trim to hold it in place. This trim will hide the stitching where you joined the wool strips to the hooked rug and any white edges of rug-backing fabric that may be visible.

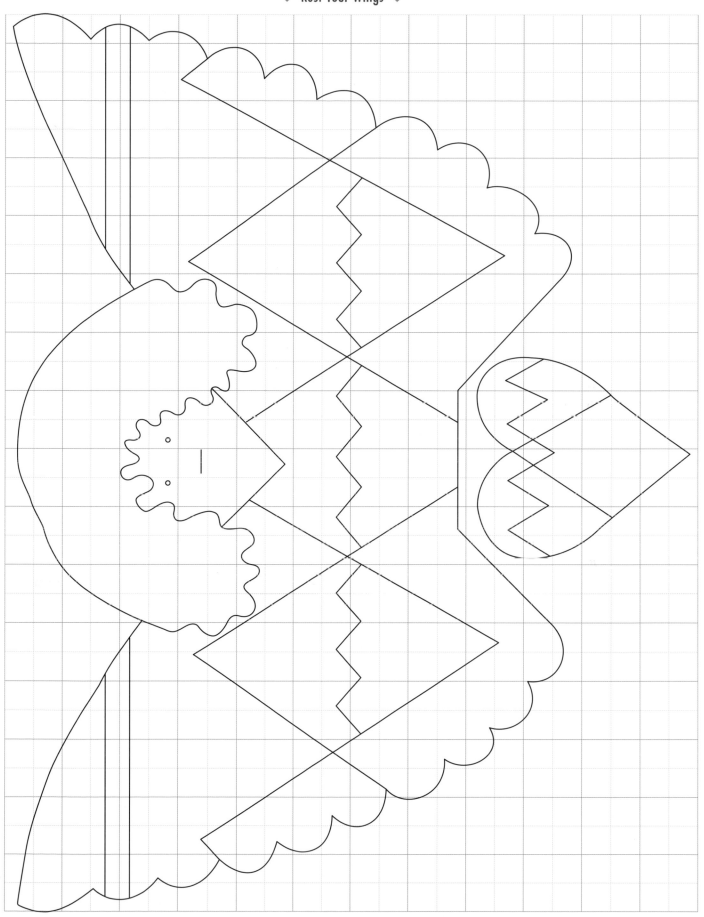

Rest Your Wings
One square equals ½".
Enlarge pattern 167% to 12" x 15½".

Polka-Dot Chickens

Hooked Rug *by Polly Minick*

Polly has created a variety of chicken-themed rugs during her career as a rug-hooking artist, but these girls are her first purple chickens! Purple is a more recent addition to Polly's color palette, and sometimes it's fun to break away from the expected and see what happens. Here, she used about nine different purple wools and then added highlights of orange, gold, and even a bit of bright blue in the whimsical scalloped border.

Finished size: 37" x 15"

Materials

Wool yardage is based on 60"-wide wool (before washing). Amounts allow for four times the area to be hooked. Please allow extra wool if you hook high loops or tend to pack your loops close together. This rug was hooked with size 8 strips.

- ¼ yard *each* of 3 different medium purple wools for the chickens and border

- ½ yard of dark purple wool for the background

- ⅛ yard or scraps of dark purple wool for wings

- 8 strips of mustard wool for the feet, combs, and beaks

- 8 strips of orange wool (or contrasting color) for the polka dots

- 6 to 8 strips *each* of at least 5 additional purple wools for the border

- 6 to 8 strips *each* of orange, gold, and bright blue wools for the border

- 23" x 45" piece of rug-backing fabric (31" x 53" if using a hoop)

- ½ yard of poplin fabric for binding (or other tightly woven heavy-duty fabric)

- Red Dot Tracer

- Black permanent marker

Cutting

Cut the assorted wools into size 8 strips. You may want to cut as you go so that you won't risk having your narrow strips tangle together.

Hooking the Rug

1. Enlarge the patterns on pages 38 and 39 as indicated. Then transfer the pattern onto your rug-backing fabric. For details on transferring patterns, see page 22.

2. Hook the polka dots; then outline each body and wing. Finally, fill in each portion using the same wool used for the outline.

CHANGING YOUR MIND

If you're not sure what color to make your polka dots, don't worry. Hook those areas anyway and fill in the chicken color around them. If you change your mind, you can always pull out the polka-dot loops and switch to another color. This is much easier than trying to hook neatly around the drawn circles and then deciding what color to make the dots.

3. Hook the beaks, combs, and feet with the mustard wool. Note that the feet are just one strip wide.

4. Hook the border line between the background and the scalloped border. Fill in the background with dark purple. Even though the background uses only one wool, you can make it more interesting (both to hook and to look at) by hooking around the chickens and then filling in the remaining areas rather than hooking it in straight lines.

5. Hook each scallop by choosing a shade of purple for the outline and switching colors as you work your way toward the center.

Finishing

Because the perimeter of the rug is scalloped, it is easier to finish the edges with a fabric facing rather than rug-binding tape or yarn.

1. To face the edges, lay the ½ yard of poplin fabric on top of your rug with right sides facing. Pin the fabric to the rug.

2. On the wrong side of the rug, machine stitch around the shape of the rug, sewing as close as possible to the edge of the rug.

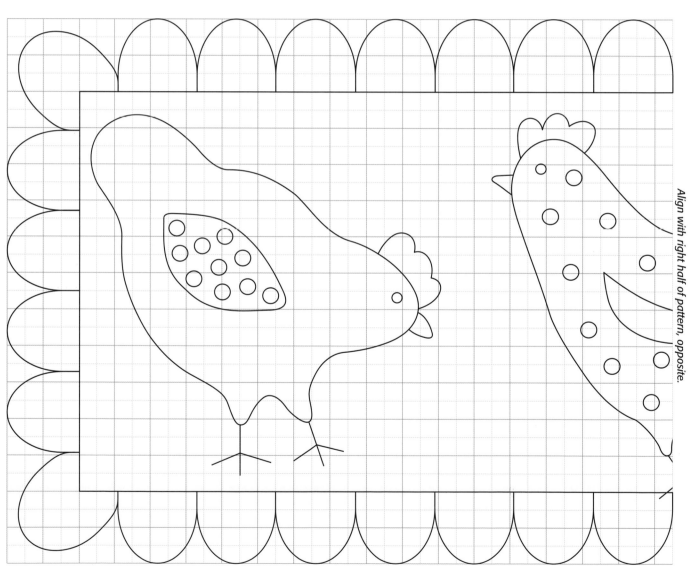

Align with right half of pattern, opposite.

Polka-Dot Chickens
One square equals ½".
Enlarge pattern 200%, and then 133%
(266% total) to 37" x 15".

3. Trim the excess facing and rug-backing fabric outside of the stitching line so that you have about a ¼" to ½" seam allowance. Clip the curves and into the points on the facing fabric only so that they won't pucker when the facing is turned. Then carefully trim away the center portion of the facing fabric, leaving about 3" of facing around the perimeter.

4. Turn the facing to the back side of the rug, turn under the raw edges, and stitch them in place to the rug backing fabric.

5. Block your finished rug, referring to page 26.

6. If desired, make a fabric label for the back of your rug and whipstitch it in place.

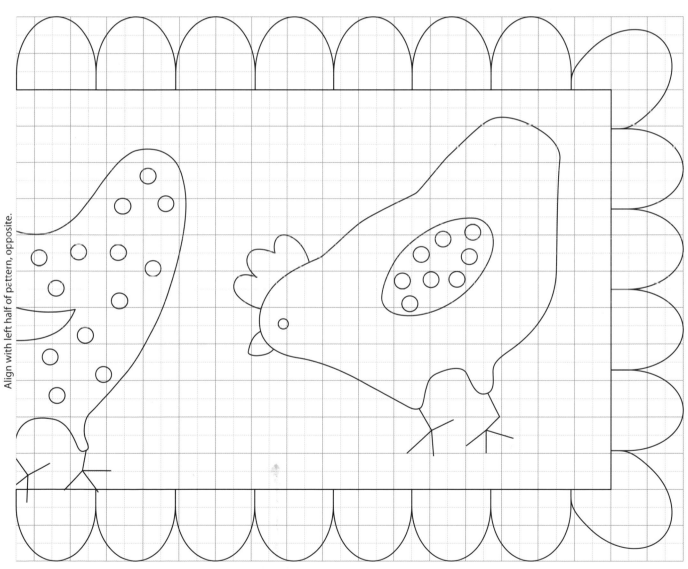

Align with left half of pattern, opposite.

Live Simply

The message on this table mat is one that many folk artists like to live by. Re-creating Tammy's primitive bouquet of flowers will give you a chance to work with soft and fluffy wool, stitching it by hand—a perfect way to slow down and enjoy some quiet, relaxing moments. And when you've finished this piece, you'll have a lasting reminder to take it easy and enjoy nature's beauty around you.

Finished size: 28" x 22"

Materials

Wool yardage is based on 60"-wide wool (before washing).

- ¾ yard of gray wool for the background
- ⅓ yard of rusty red wool for the flowerpot
- ¼ yard or 5" x 10" square of coral wool #1 for flowers
- ⅛ yard *each* of coral wools #2 and #3 for the flowers
- ⅛ yard or 6" x 6" square *each* of dark red wools #1 and #2 for the flowers
- ⅛ yard *each* of green wools #1 and #2 for the stems and leaves
- ⅛ yard of cream wool for the banner
- ⅛ yard of dark olive wool for the banner pole
- ⅛ yard of dark brown or gray wool for the banner letters
- ⅛ yard of chartreuse wool for the flowerpot accents
- ⅓ yard of red striped cotton fabric for the binding
- ¾ yard of flannel, wool, or cotton for the backing
- Freezer paper
- Lightweight fusible web
- Embroidery floss in colors to match the appliqués

Cutting

Trace the patterns on pages 44 and 45 onto the dull side of freezer paper. Cut the shapes outside of the traced lines. Iron the freezer-paper shapes onto the right side of the appropriate-colored wool and cut them out on the drawn lines.

From the gray wool, cut:
1 rectangle, 22" x 28"

From the rusty red wool, cut:
1 flowerpot

From the dark olive wool, cut:
1 strip, ⅜" x 13"

From the cream wool, cut:
1 banner

From green wool #1, cut:
1 stem, 5/16" x 5½"
2 stems, 5/16" x 6"
2 stems, 5/16" x 10"

From the chartreuse wool, cut:
4 circles
4 short stripes
1 long stripe
3 strips, ¼" x 2½"

From green wool #2, cut:
2 of leaf D
8 of leaf E

From coral wool #1, cut:
1 of outer flower A
7 of flower C

From dark red wool #1, cut:
1 of inner flower A

From dark red wool #2, cut:
2 of outer flower B

From coral wool #2, cut:
2 of inner flower B
5 of flower C

From coral wool #3, cut:
6 of flower C

From the dark brown or gray wool, cut:
Live Simply letters

From the backing fabric, cut:
1 rectangle, 22" x 28"

From the striped binding fabric, cut:
3 strips, 3½" x width of fabric

Making the Table Mat

1. Position the flowerpot on the gray wool, centering the flowerpot 1½" from the bottom edge. Do not stitch yet. Lay out the dark olive strip for

the banner pole and the cream banner to find a pleasing placement. The end of the pole will tuck under the flowerpot. Using two strands of matching embroidery floss, appliqué the banner and pole using a blanket stitch. See page 15 for blanket-stitch instructions.

2. Position the five stems, referring to the project photograph for placement. The shortest stem goes in the center for the A flower, the next shortest are for the B flowers, and the longest stems are on the ends for the C flowers. Whipstitch the stems in place using one strand of matching embroidery floss. See page 15 for whipstitch instructions.

3. Appliqué the flowerpot accents in place to the flowerpot using two strands of matching embroidery floss and a blanket stitch. Appliqué the flowerpot in place in the same way.

4. Appliqué a D leaf to the top of each B flower stem using one strand of embroidery floss and a blanket stitch. In the same manner, stitch four E leaves to the A flower stem and two E leaves to each B flower stem, referring to the project photo for placement.

5. Using one strand of matching floss and a blanket stitch, appliqué the outer section of the A flower at the top of the center stem. Appliqué the inner section of the A flower in the same manner. To complete the A flower, position the three chartreuse strips on the inner section of the flower, referring to the project photo on page 40 for placement. Whipstitch the strips in place one at a time using one strand of floss.

6. Blanket-stitch the dark red outer sections of the B flowers at the top of the stems using one strand of floss. Add the coral inner sections of the B flowers in the same manner.

7. Position nine C flower pieces along each of the remaining stems. Blanket-stitch them in place using one strand of floss.

8. Appliqué the letters to the banner using one strand of floss and a whipstitch.

Finishing

1. Tammy finds it easier to bind a wool project if the wool is stabilized with lightweight fusible web first. To do this, cut the fusible web to fit the piece of backing fabric. Iron it onto the wrong side of the backing fabric.

2. Lay the finished appliquéd wool piece face down on your ironing board. Remove the paper backing from the fusible web and place the backing piece wrong side down on the appliquéd wool piece so that the wrong sides of the appliqué top and fused backing are facing. Iron in place according to the manufacturer's instructions.

3. Sew the three striped binding strips together end to end to make one long strip. Lay the binding strip on the wool piece, right sides together. Using a ¾"-wide seam allowance, begin stitching about 1" from the end of the binding strip. Stop stitching ¾" from the corner of the wool piece. Remove the work from the machine, fold the binding up and then back down as shown so that it is in line with the next edge of the wool piece. This forms a mitered binding corner. Stitch along this side of the project, stopping ¾" from the corner. Repeat the same process at each corner.

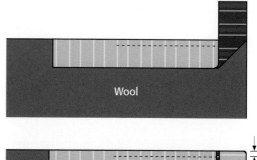

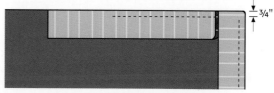

4. When you are nearing the starting point, stop stitching and fold back the 1" of binding that was left unsewn in the beginning. Lay the other end of the binding strip on top of the beginning tail

and continue stitching approximately 1" past the starting point.

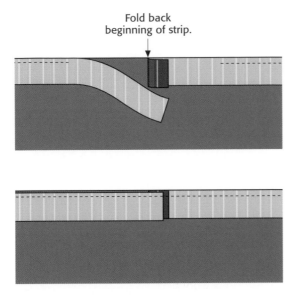

Fold back beginning of strip.

5. Trim the excess binding. Fold the raw edge of the binding to the back side of the project. Turn under ¾" and whipstitch the folded edge in place.

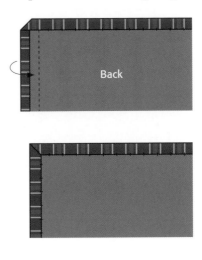

Back

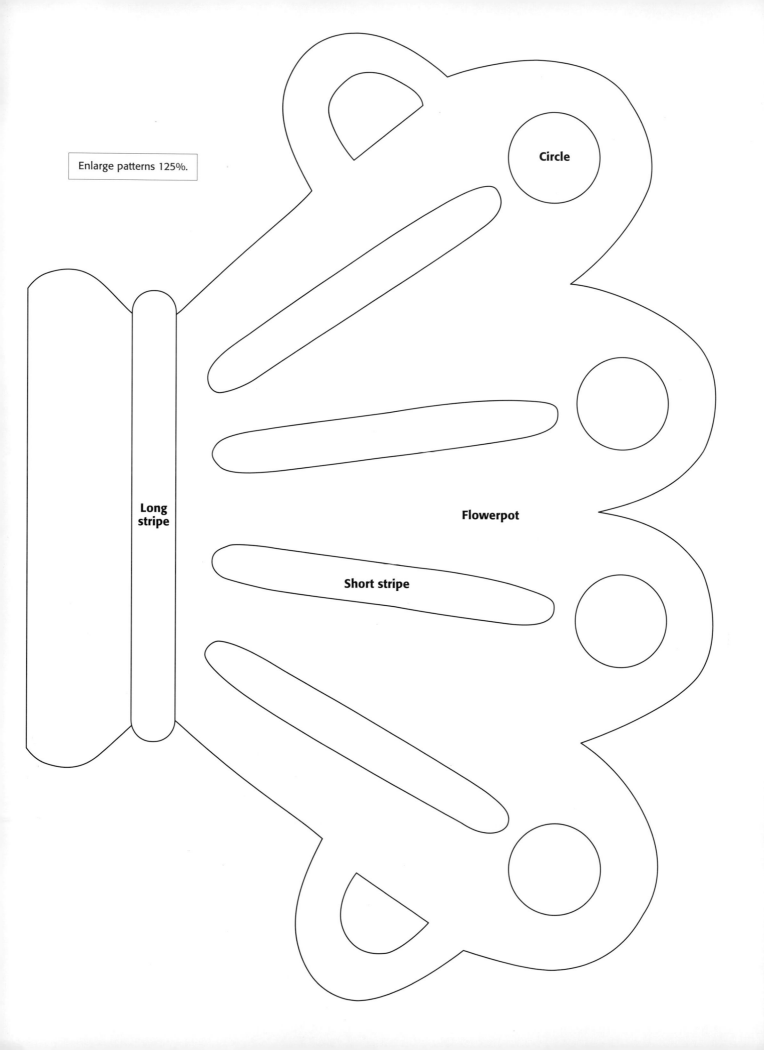

Enlarge patterns 125%.

Circle

Long stripe

Flowerpot

Short stripe

Outer flower A

Inner flower A

Live Simply

Enlarge banner patterns 150%.

Flower C

Flower and leaf patterns are full-size.

Leaf E

Leaf D

Outer flower B

Inner flower B

45

"C" Is for Cat

Hooked Rug *by Avis Shirer of Joined at the Hip*

This sampler rug combines many of Avis's favorite things: one of her cats, the American flag, and colorful flowers. To add a primitive touch, she hooked *abc* and *123* in the design, keeping alive the spirit of embroidered alphabet samplers of days gone by.

Finished size: 25" x 19"

Materials

Wool yardage is based on 60"-wide wool (before washing). Amounts allow for four times the area to be hooked. Please allow extra wool if you hook high loops or tend to pack your loops close together. This rug was hooked with size 8 strips.

- ½ yard of cream-and-taupe plaid wool for the cat background

- ¼ yard of light green wool for the *abc* background, *123* background, and stems

- ¼ yard of off-white wool for the letters, numbers, cat eyes, and flag stripes

- ¼ yard of brown wool for the border and outlines between hooked sections

- ¼ yard of antique black wool for the cat and the word *CAT*

- ¼ yard of red wool for the flag and Log Cabin squares

- ¼ yard of medium blue wool for the word *CAT* background

- ⅛ yard *each* or scraps of 2 bright pink wools for the flowers and cat nose

- ⅛ yard *each* or scraps of dark rose and light rose for the flowers

- ⅛ yard of medium green wool for the leaves

- ⅛ yard or scraps of yellow wool for the flower centers

- ⅛ yard of dark blue wool for the flag

- Scraps of assorted colors of wool for the Log Cabin squares

- 27" x 33" piece of rug-backing fabric (35" x 41" if using a hoop)

- 3 yards of rug-binding tape

- 3 yards of ¼"-diameter cotton cording

- 30 yards of dark brown 3-ply wool yarn for whip-stitching edges

- Red Dot Tracer

- Black permanent marker

Cutting

Cut the assorted wools into size 8 strips. You may want to cut as you go so that you won't risk having your narrow strips tangle together.

Hooking the Rug

1. Enlarge the pattern on page 49 as indicated. Then transfer the pattern onto your rug-backing fabric. For details on transferring patterns, see page 22.

2. Using the brown wool, hook the outlines that divide the pattern into its various sections.

3. Outline the cat head with antique black wool. Hook the eyes with off-white wool and the nose with the lightest bright pink wool. Fill in the head with antique black wool. Finally, outline the cat body with antique black wool and fill it in using the same color.

4. Hook the flower stems with light green and the leaves with medium green wool. Hook all of the flower centers with yellow wool. Hook two of the flowers with both bright pink wools and two with the two shades of rose wools.

5. Fill in the background behind the cat and flowers with the taupe-and-cream plaid wool.

6. Hook *abc* and *123* with off-white wool. Fill in the backgrounds of these two sections with light green wool.

7. For the Log Cabin squares, start at the outer edge of each and hook three concentric rounds using assorted colors of wool. Then fill in the center of each block with red wool.

8. Hook the word *CAT* with antique black wool. Fill in the background of this section with medium blue wool.

9. Hook the blue field of the flag using the dark blue wool. Then hook the red and off-white stripes to complete the flag.

10. Using brown wool, hook four rows around the perimeter of the rug for the border.

Finishing

1. Block your finished rug, referring to page 26.

2. Finish the edges of the rug. The rug shown has cording inserted around the edges that is then whipstitched in place with wool yarn. See page 27 for instructions on making a corded edge. Finish it off with rug-binding tape on the back of the rug.

3. If desired, make a fabric label for the back of your rug and whipstitch it in place.

"C" Is for Cat
One square equals ½".
Enlarge pattern 200%, and then 125%
(250% total) to 17¼" x 23¼".

Geometric Gussets

Hooked Purse *by Nola A. Heidbreder*

Here's a chance to take your hooking with you wherever you go! This fun little purse is hooked flat, just like any hooked rug, and then the sides are stitched together by hand. A wool lining, magnetic clasp, and leather handle make this handbag not only useful but quite stylish, too.

Finished size of purse: 12" x 5" x 2"
Finished size of hooking: 12½" x 12"

Materials

Wool yardage is based on 60"-wide wool (before washing). Amounts allow for four times the area to be hooked. Please allow extra wool if you hook high loops or tend to pack your loops close together. This purse was hooked with size 8 strips.

- ½ yard *total* of wool in assorted hot colors: bright orange, dull orange, violet, blue-violet, red-violet, and red

- 13" x 13½" piece of magenta wool for the lining

- 20" x 20" piece of rug-backing fabric (28" x 28" if using a hoop)

- Sewing thread to match lining

- 50" of binding tape

- 12 yards of dark purple or black 3-ply wool yarn for whipstitched edges

- 38"-long black leather strap and findings

- ½"-diameter magnetic snap

- Red Dot Tracer

- Black permanent marker

Cutting

Cut the assorted wools into size 8 strips. You may want to cut as you go so that you won't risk having your narrow strips tangle together. *Do not* cut the magenta wool for the lining into strips.

Hooking the Purse

1. Enlarge the pattern on page 53 as indicated. Then transfer the pattern onto your rug-backing fabric. For details on transferring patterns, see page 22.

2. Hook the diamonds on the purse bottom with the brighter colors. Hook the outside of the diamonds first and work toward the centers, alternating colors as you go. Use the duller colors for the triangles on the purse bottom to make the diamonds really stand out.

3. Hook the shapes on the front and back of the purse. Fill in the shapes, alternating colors. Then hook around the shapes, again alternating colors.

Finishing

1. Block the hooked piece, referring to page 26.

2. Whipstitch around all edges of the hooked piece with the wool yarn and add binding tape. See pages 26 and 27 for whipstitching and binding techniques.

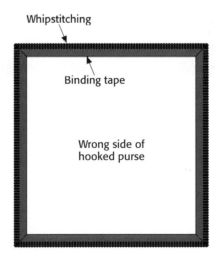

Whipstitching

Binding tape

Wrong side of hooked purse

3. Lay the hooked purse face down on your table. Lay the lining fabric on top of it, right side up, so that ½" of the lining fabric extends beyond each edge of the purse. Fold under ½" of the lining fabric along the purse sides and pin in place. Then fold

under ½" on the top and bottom edges of the lining and pin. The folded lining edges should fall just under the whipstitched edges of the purse.

Wool lining

Pin lining in place
just inside whipstitched edges.

4. Before stitching the lining to the purse, insert the two halves of the snap, one on each top inside edge of the purse, 1" down from the top whipstitching. Be sure that each half is centered so that the two will line up for closing the purse. Refer to the instructions that came with your snap for installing it properly.

5. Hand stitch the lining to the binding tape with sewing thread; stitch just under the whipstitching.

6. Mark the two fold lines (see the pattern) on each side of the purse with pins. Then, with the right sides of the hooked purse together, fold the purse at these markings and sew the front and back side edges together with the wool yarn. Do not knot the yarn. Starting at the top edge, run the yarn tail under the bound edge of the purse several times and then begin sewing the sides together, working toward the bottom of the purse.

7. Stitch for about 4", to the point where you need to make the gusset that will form the bottom of the purse. Use the pin markings as your guide. The gusset will look like an inverted T at the bottom of the purse. To form the gusset, push the bottom of the purse firmly against a tabletop. The pins should be straight across from one another. Continue stitching with the wool yarn, first out one arm of the T and then back again toward the center. Then stitch the other arm of the T and back toward the center to finish the gusset. To secure

the yarn, stitch about ½" back up the side of the purse and run the yarn under the stitched edge before clipping it off. Repeat for the other side of the purse.

Inside lining

Stitch gusset in place.

BE FIRM!

When stitching the sides and gussets of your purse, pull firmly on the yarn to bring the bound edges as close together as possible. This will make your purse structurally sound and prevent gaps between the rows of hooking at the purse sides.

8. Nola used a purchased leather handle with metal rings attached at the ends. Hand sew these rings in place at the top of each side seam using the wool yarn. See "Resources" on page 91 for handle information.

Whipstitch metal rings at side seams.

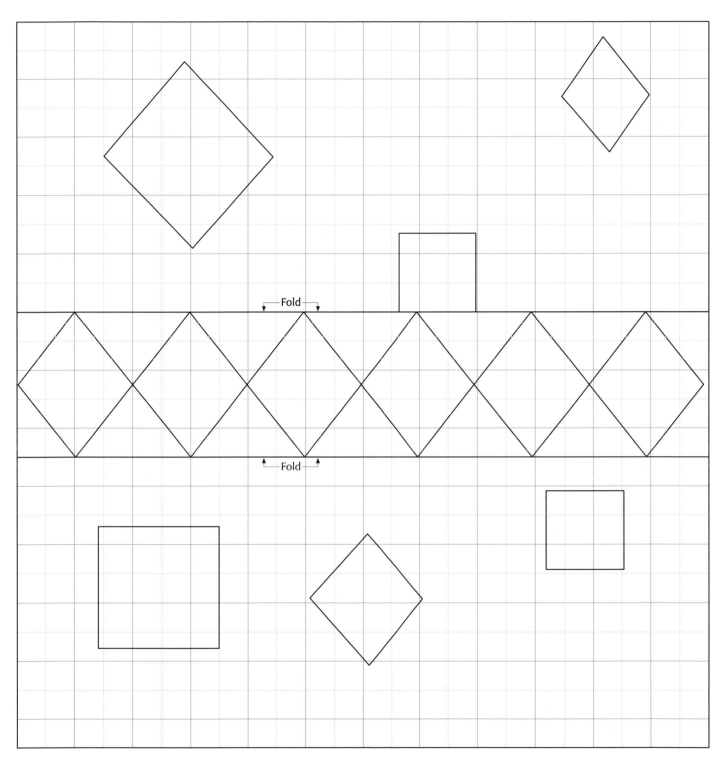

Geometric Gussets Purse
One square equals ½".
Enlarge pattern 167% to 12" x 12½".

Impressionistic Diamonds

Hooked Purse *by Nola A. Heidbreder*

This little bag is a perfect project for using up leftover strips from other wool projects. Nola used a rainbow of colors in lights and darks, both bright and dull, for a purse that will look good with just about any outfit in your closet. As a finishing touch, easy crocheted granny squares are joined to create the purse sides and thrift-store beaded necklaces make sparkling straps. If you prefer, you could bead your own handles.

Finished size of purse: 9" x 5" x 3"
Finished size of hooking: 9" x 13"

Materials

Wool yardage is based on 60"-wide wool (before washing). Amounts allow for four times the area to be hooked. Please allow extra wool if you hook high loops or tend to pack your loops close together. This purse was hooked with size 4 strips.

- ¼ yard *total* of wool in assorted colors: lights, darks, dulls, and brights

- 13" x 15" piece of light green wool for the lining

- 17" x 21" piece of rug-backing fabric (25" x 29" if using a hoop)

- Sewing thread to match lining

- 46" of binding tape

- 10 yards of black wool yarn for whipstitched edges

- 1 skein or scraps of variegated worsted-weight wool yarn for Granny Squares (Nola used Manos del Uruguay yarn)

- Two 20"-long beaded necklaces

- ½"-diameter gold-tone magnetic snap

- Size J crochet hook

- Red Dot Tracer

- Black permanent marker

Cutting

From the light green wool for lining, cut:
    1 rectangle, 8¾" x 15"
    2 rectangles, 3¾" x 6¾"

From the assorted wools, cut:
    Size 4 strips. Separate the strips into piles of light, bright, dull, and dark. You may want to cut as you go so that you won't risk having your narrow strips tangle together.

Hooking the Purse

1. Enlarge the pattern on page 57 as indicated. Then transfer the pattern onto your rug-backing fabric. For details on transferring patterns, see page 22.

2. Using dark strips, hook the border all the way around the purse. Don't be afraid to mix and match colors; the color *value* is what will form the design.

3. Again using dark strips, hook the outside lines of all the wavy diamonds. Using bright strips, hook the inside lines of the wavy diamonds. Then hook the areas within the lines, alternating the dull strips with the light strips until each diamond is complete.

Crocheting the Granny Squares

If you've never crocheted, try it—Nola says most rug hookers learn quickly because the hooking motion is essentially the same. See page 29 for illustrations and instructions.

1. Chain 4, join with a slip stitch to form a ring.

2. Chain 3 and then make 2 double crochets in the ring. Chain 3, *make 3 double crochets in the ring, chain 3, repeat from * twice. Join with a slip stitch into the third stitch of the beginning chain-3. The first round of the granny square is complete.

3. Chain 3, and in the same chain-3 space, make 2 double crochets, chain 3, and make 3 double crochets. *Chain 1, and in the next chain-3 space from the first round, make 3 double crochets, chain 3, make 3 double crochets, repeat from * twice more. Chain 1 and join with a slip stitch to the third stitch of the beginning chain 3. Fasten off.

4. Repeat to make a total of four granny squares. Using the same yarn, whipstitch the granny squares together in pairs to make the two sides of the purse. Set aside.

Finishing

1. Block the purse, referring to page 26.

2. Whipstitch around all edges of the purse with the wool yarn and add binding tape to them as well. See pages 26 and 27 for binding techniques.

3. Pin the granny square sides in place, starting at the top so that the top edges of the purse front, purse back, and granny square side are all even. Hand sew the crochet to the whipstitched edges of the purse front, back, and bottom. Repeat for the other side of the purse.

Variegated wool granny squares add rich color and texture to the sides of this purse.

4. To make the lining, round off the two corners on one end of each of the 3¾" x 6¾" light green rectangles. You can use a saucer or glass to mark the corners or simply cut them freehand. Then machine stitch one long edge of the 8¾" x 15" rectangle to one of these pieces as shown, using a ½"-wide seam allowance. Ease gently as you sew around the curve. Repeat to sew the other rounded-off rectangle to the other long edge of the lining rectangle.

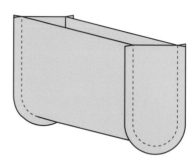

5. Insert the two halves of the snap, one on each top inside edge of the purse, 1" down from the top whipstitching. Be sure that each half is centered so that they will line up for closing the purse. Refer to the instructions that came with your snap for installing it properly.

6. Insert the lining into the purse, wrong sides together. (The seams on the lining should be facing the inside of the purse.) Fold under ½" all the way around the top edge of the lining and pin in place along the top of the purse, just beneath the whipstitched edge. The edges of the larger rectangle should match the front and back of the purse and the smaller rectangles should align with the top edges of the sides of the purse. Hand stitch the lining to the binding tape with sewing thread; stitch just under the whipstitching.

7. Hand stitch the beaded necklaces to the top outside edges of the purse to form the purse straps.

Impressionistic Diamonds Purse
One square equals ½".
Enlarge pattern 150% to 9" x 13".

Winter Wool

Table Mat and Stocking *by Linda Lenich and Jennifer Zoeterman of Pure Wool*

Linda and Jennifer's clever technique for cutting wool rickrack with a wave-edge rotary-cutting blade combined with dimensional berries makes this pair of wintry projects a real standout. The berries are applied using needle felting, while the rest of the motifs are stitched by hand. Use the table mat to decorate your dining room table or a coffee table, and hang the stocking on a door.

Finished mat size: 18" x 14" oval

Table-Mat Materials

- Fat quarter of light green wool for the table mat
- Fat quarter of red wool for the table-mat backing
- Fat quarter of brown wool for the rickrack vine
- Several scraps (at least 4" x 4" each) of assorted green wools for the holly leaves
- Small piece of 100%-wool roving/fleece in variegated pinks and reds (Pure Wool's 100%-merino-wool fleece in the colorway Red Rapture)
- Hand-felting needle
- 8" x 8" square of 2"-thick foam for needle felting
- Rotary cutter with scallop and wave blades
- Size 8 pearl cotton in shades of green and brown
- Size 22 chenille needle
- Freezer paper

Making the Table Mat

Using the patterns on pages 61–63, make freezer-paper templates for the mat top, mat backing, and the holly leaves (three large, five medium, two small, and three extra-small).

1. Using a dry iron on the wool setting, press the mat-top template to the wrong side of the light green wool. Using a scallop-blade rotary cutter, cut out

the wool along the outside edge of the marked line. In the same manner, press the mat-backing template to the back of the red wool. Cut along the outer edge of the marked line with the scallop rotary-cutter blade.

2. Change the blade on your rotary cutter to the wave blade and cut four 18"-long pieces of brown wool for rickrack. See "Making Waves" below for tips on creating your own wool rickrack.

MAKING WAVES

Cutting strips with a wave blade isn't a precise science. Use a long rotary-cutting ruler as a guide to help you keep on the straight of grain. But don't press the rotary cutter right against the ruler as you would do with a straight-blade cutter or you'll risk nicking the ruler or damaging the blade.

First, position the ruler along one straight edge of the wool and cut off this straight edge with the wavy blade. Then move the ruler over ¼", measuring from the peak of the wave. To make the next cut, try to align the rotary blade so that the peaks of the waves will match up and form a zigzag strip that resembles rickrack. The waves may not stay perfectly aligned as you cut; simply choose the four best cuts to use as vines for your project.

3. Referring to the photograph for placement, position the brown wool rickrack on the light green oval. (Note that four lengths are used and that the ends are hidden under the large cluster of holly leaves.) Trim as needed and pin the rickrack in place. Using brown pearl cotton, stitch the rickrack in place as shown, taking a long, straight stitch over the rickrack from one valley of a wave to the next valley on the opposite side.

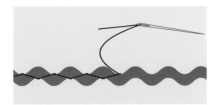

4. Turn iron to the "wool" setting, and then press the freezer-paper templates for the holly leaves onto the scraps of assorted green wools. Use scissors to cut out each leaf along the marked line. Position the holly leaves, referring to the photograph for placement, and pin in place. Using green pearl cotton and a stem stitch, stitch each leaf in place through the center. (See page 15 for stem-stitch details.) The stitching will give the look of veins in the leaves. Leave the edges free. For the largest leaves, sew additional veins from the center vein to each point of the leaves.

Stem stitch leaves in place.

5. Create the berries by pulling a small amount of fleece from the end of the round. Loosely gather it into a small ball with your fingers or palms and place in the desired position on the green wool mat. Place the green mat on the foam, and then push the felting needle through the center of the fleece ball and green wool top a few times to hold it in place. Then needle around the edge of the circle to define the circle shape and size. Continue to needle the fleece berry until it is completely held in place. Finished berries have firm edges with very few stray fibers. For detailed instructions on needle felting, see page 17.

6. Continue adding berries of various colors and sizes. Notice on the project shown that some of the berries are needle felted to the light green mat while others are on top of the leaves.

7. After all stitching and needle felting is complete, center the light green mat top on the red oval backing and pin in place. Using green pearl cotton and a running stitch, sew the mat top to the backing, stitching ¼" from the scalloped edge.

Finished stocking size: approximately 9½" x 15½"

Stocking Materials

- Fat quarter of medium green wool for the stocking top

- Fat quarter of cream wool for the stocking middle

- Fat quarter of red wool for the stocking backing

- Fat quarter of brown wool for the rickrack vine

- Several scraps (at least 4" x 4" each) of assorted green wools for the holly leaves

- Small piece of 100%-wool roving/fleece in variegated pinks and reds (Linda and Jennifer used Pure Wool's 100%-merino-wool fleece in the colorways Red Rapture and The Classics)

- Hand-felting needle

- 8" x 8" square of 2"-thick foam for needle felting

- Rotary cutter with scallop and wave blades

- Size 8 pearl cotton in shades of green and brown to match the wools

- Size 22 chenille needle

- Freezer paper

Making the Stocking

Using the patterns on page 63, make freezer-paper templates for the stocking top, stocking middle, stocking backing, and the holly leaves (two medium, three small, and two extra-small).

1. Using a dry iron on the wool setting, press the stocking-top template to the wrong side of the medium green wool. Using a rotary cutter with a scallop blade, cut out the wool along the outside edge of the marked line. In the same manner, press the stocking-backing template on the wrong side of the red wool. Cut along the outside edge of the marked line with the scallop rotary-cutter blade.

2. Press the stocking-middle template to the wrong side of the cream wool. Use scissors to cut out this shape on the marked line.

3. Change the blade of your rotary cutter to the wave blade and cut one 18"-long piece of brown wool for rickrack. See "Making Waves" on page 59 for details.

4. Referring to the photograph on page 60 for placement, position the brown wool rickrack on the medium green stocking. Trim as needed and pin the rickrack in place. Using brown pearl cotton, stitch the rickrack in place as shown, taking a long, straight stitch over the rickrack from one valley of a wave to the next valley on the opposite side.

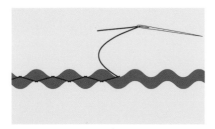

5. Turn iron to "wool" setting, and then press the freezer-paper templates for the holly leaves on the scraps of assorted green wools. Use scissors to cut out each leaf along the marked line. Position the holly leaves, referring to the photograph for placement, and pin in place. Using green pearl cotton and a stem stitch, stitch each leaf in place through the center. The stitching will give the look of veins in the leaves. Leave the edges free. For the largest leaves, sew additional veins from the center vein to each point of the leaves. Refer to the illustration with step 4 on page 60.

6. Create the berries by pulling a small amount of fleece from the end of the round. Loosely gather it into a small ball with your fingers or palms and place in the desired position on the medium green mat. Place the green mat on the foam, and then push the felting needle through the center of the fleece ball and medium green top a few times to hold it in place. Then needle around the edge of the circle to define the circle shape and size. Continue to needle the fleece berry until it is completely held in place. Finished berries have firm edges with very few stray fibers. For detailed instructions on needle felting, see page 17.

7. Continue adding berries of various colors and sizes. Notice on the project shown that the red and pink berries are clustered by the leaves, but that a few small white berries have also been added along the brown rickrack. Also needle felt larger white dots along the top edge of the green stocking.

8. When the green stocking top is complete, center it on the cream stocking middle and pin in place. With green pearl cotton, stitch ¼" from the scalloped top of the stocking only; use a running stitch.

9. Pin the green top/cream middle onto the red stocking backing. Using a running stitch, sew through all three layers along the sides and bottom only, leaving the top open. Stitch ¼" from the green scalloped edge using green pearl cotton.

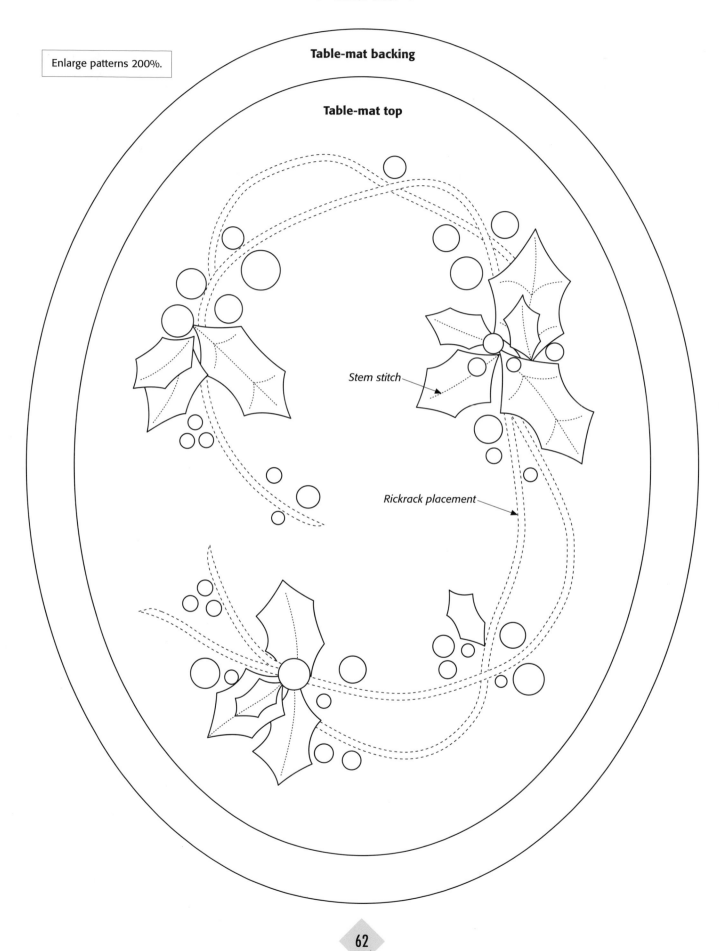

Enlarge patterns 200%.

Table-mat backing

Table-mat top

Stem stitch

Rickrack placement

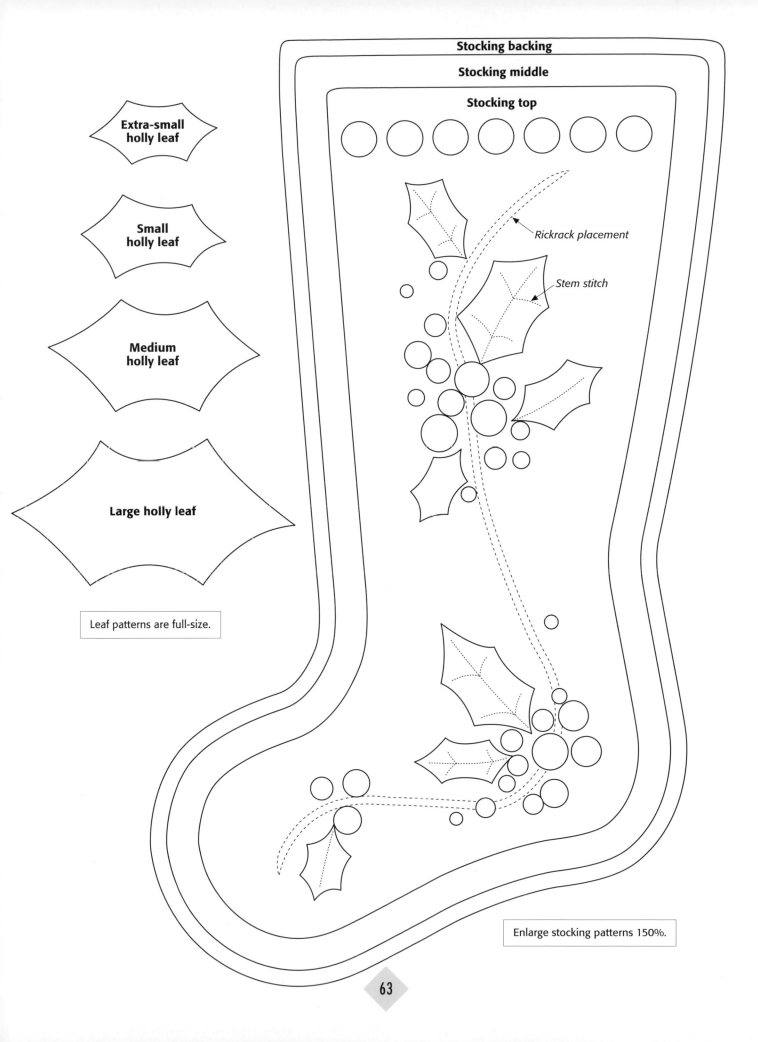

Stocking backing

Stocking middle

Stocking top

Rickrack placement

Stem stitch

Extra-small holly leaf

Small holly leaf

Medium holly leaf

Large holly leaf

Leaf patterns are full-size.

Enlarge stocking patterns 150%.

63

Hearts versus Stars

Hooked-Rug Game Board *by Wendy Miller of the Red Saltbox*

This delightful little hooked rug makes a unique gift for adults and children alike. The checkerboard rug, along with its painted matching heart and star game pieces, is a functional as well as decorative piece. When the game pieces aren't in use, tie them up in a small sack stitched from your leftover wool.

Finished size: 12" x 24"

Materials

Wool yardage is based on 60"-wide wool (before washing). Amounts allow for four times the area to be hooked. Please allow extra wool if you hook high loops or tend to pack your loops close together. This rug was hooked with size 8.5 strips.

- ⅝ yard of black wool for the checkerboard squares, stars, hearts, and outlining

- ¼ yard of mustard plaid wool for the checkerboard squares

- ⅛ yard of mustard wool for the stars background

- ⅛ yard of red wool for the hearts background

- 20" x 32" of rug-backing fabric (28" x 40" if using a hoop)

- 2⅓ yards of rug-binding tape

- Red Dot Tracer

- Black permanent marker

Materials for Game Pieces (Optional)

- 12 each of unfinished 1½" wooden stars and hearts for game pieces

- Mustard and red acrylic craft paint

- Sealer spray in matte finish

- Paintbrush

Cutting

Cut the assorted wools into size 8 or 8.5 strips. You may want to cut as you go so that you won't risk having your narrow strips tangle together.

Hooking the Game Board

1. Enlarge the pattern on page 67 as indicated. Then transfer the pattern onto your rug-backing fabric. For details on transferring patterns, see page 22.

2. Hook the outline of the rug with black wool, keeping the corners as clean and sharp as you can. Also hook one row of black wool between the center checkerboard and the star and heart sections.

3. Starting in one corner of the center checkerboard area and working across the first row, hook the checkerboard squares, alternating between black and plaid wool squares. Work your way across the board, hooking a black square, then a plaid square, then a black square, and so on. Hook each individual square by outlining the square shape first, and then filling it in. Take care to keep your outlines inside the marked lines so that your squares stay uniform in size.

4. Hook the stars and hearts in black wool. Remember to outline them first to hold the shape, and then fill them in.

5. Hook the background behind the stars with the mustard wool.

6. Hook the background behind the hearts with the red wool.

Finishing

1. Block your finished rug, referring to page 26.

2. Finish your rug using binding tape. See page 26 for binding techniques.

3. If desired, make a fabric label for the back of your rug and whipstitch it in place.

Making the Optional Game Pieces

1. Paint your star game pieces with mustard acrylic craft paint and let dry.

2. Paint your heart game pieces with red acrylic craft paint and let dry.

3. Spray your game pieces with matte sealer spray and let dry. Turn over the game pieces and spray the other side and let dry.

An as-is check wool was the starting point for this checkerboard rug. Wendy combined it with a black, a windowpane plaid overdyed dark red, and a herringbone weave overdyed mustard.

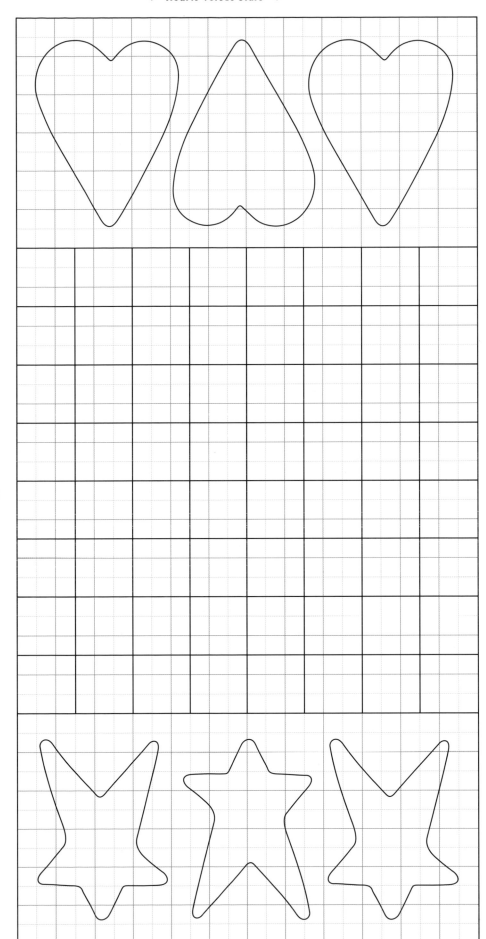

Hearts versus Stars
One square equals ½".
Enlarge pattern 200%,
and then 125% (250% total)
to 12" x 24".

Indian Summer

Picnic Basket with Hooked Lid *by Donna C. Lever*

When Donna saw this old twill picnic basket with a missing lid for sale in a local antique shop, she knew it would be a perfect candidate for a hooked top. If you have a basket with different dimensions, you may need to adjust the pattern slightly. Or you could simply hook the pattern and use it as an oval table mat.

Finished size: 19½" x 11½" oval

Materials

Wool yardage is based on 60"-wide wool (before washing). Amounts allow for four times the area to be hooked. Please allow extra wool if you hook high loops or tend to pack your loops close together. This basket top was hooked with size 8 strips.

- ¼ yard *each* of red, purple, green, and gold wools for the background stripes
- ¼ yard *total* of assorted orange wools for the center pumpkin
- ¼ yard *total* of assorted rusty brown wools for the medium pumpkin
- ¼ yard *total* of assorted yellowish orange wools for the small pumpkin
- ¼ yard of mottled cream wool for the background
- ⅛ yard of grayish green wool for the pumpkin stems
- ⅛ yard of dark olive wool for the diamond and stripe outlines
- 20" x 28" piece of rug-backing fabric (28" x 36" if using a hoop)
- 2 yards of ½"-wide braided edging
- ½ yard of cotton quilt batting
- Freezer paper or butcher paper
- Strong glue, suitable for wood and fabric (Donna used Crafter's Pick "The Ultimate!")
- 2 pieces of ¼" birch plywood cut to fit the top of your basket
- 1 piece of cardboard to fit the top of your basket
- Craft paint or stain
- Red Dot Tracer
- Black permanent marker

Cutting

Cut the assorted wools into size 8 strips. You may want to cut as you go so that you won't risk having your narrow strips tangle together.

Hooking the Lid

1. Using butcher paper or freezer paper, turn your basket upside down and trace the outside of the opening. Enlarge the pattern on page 71 to fit the paper basket-top pattern. (The pattern given was enlarged 200% to fit the basket shown.) Transfer the design onto your rug-backing fabric. For details on transferring patterns, see page 22.

2. Hook the pumpkins, starting with the large center pumpkin in the background and then hooking the smaller pumpkins. For each pumpkin, use the darkest of your assorted oranges, rusty browns, or yellowish oranges to hook the curved accent lines. Then fill in the remainder of the pumpkin, hooking in curved vertical lines to mimick the shape of the pumpkin. Hook the stems using the grayish green wool and the tendrils using green wool (the green will also be used for the stripes).

3. Hook the diamond outline using the dark olive wool. Using the same color, hook the outlines between the red, green, gold, and purple stripes.

4. Fill in the diamond shape using the mottled cream wool strips.

5. Fill in the stripes around the perimeter of the rug. Start by hooking the red stripes closest to the center. Then work your way toward the ends of the basket topper, hooking one quadrant at a time.

6. Block the finished rug, referring to page 26 as needed. Trim the excess backing fabric so that you have about 2" remaining. Fold this fabric to the back of the rug and press.

Preparing the Basket Top

1. Using the same paper pattern as you used for the perimeter of the hooked rug, cut a piece of ¼" plywood the exact size of basket. Cut a second piece of plywood ¼" smaller than the *inside* edge of your basket. Sand the edges of both pieces and then paint or stain them. After they've dried, glue the two pieces together, taking care to center the smaller piece on the bottom of the larger piece. *Note:* Your basket may be slightly irregular shaped, so make sure that you glue the small piece to the bottom of the larger piece. Otherwise, your top may not fit as well as you'd like.

2. Cut a piece of cardboard the same size as the basket top. Cut five pieces of batting the same size as the cardboard. Then trim ½" all the way around one piece, trim 1" off the second piece, and trim 1½" from the last two pieces. Glue the batting to the cardboard, starting with the largest piece of batting. End with the smallest piece of batting on top.

3. Center the rug over the batting side of the cardboard and double check the fit. Starting on one long side, apply glue to the cardboard and fold the linen backing to the cardboard side and hold in place until the glue holds. Check to make sure the rug looks even on the right side—be sure the edges are as tight as possible so

that no linen shows. Glue the second long side in the same manner, and finish by gluing the ends in place, easing the excess fabric around the curves.

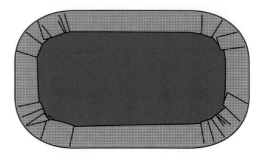

Glue linen edges to cardboard,
pleating at the curves to ease excess fabric.

4. Starting at one short end of the basket top, glue the braid to the back of the rug. Leave about a 3" tail of braid at the starting point so that you can overlap or weave the ends together once the braid is all the way around the rug. Place a thin bead of glue around the edge of the cardboard and then lay the flat part of the braid on the glue and hold in place until the glue sets.

5. Glue the rug to the wood cover. The braid should overlap the edge of the wood a little bit. Place a heavy book or two on top of the rug until the glue has dried. Sign and date the inside of the lid with a permanent marker.

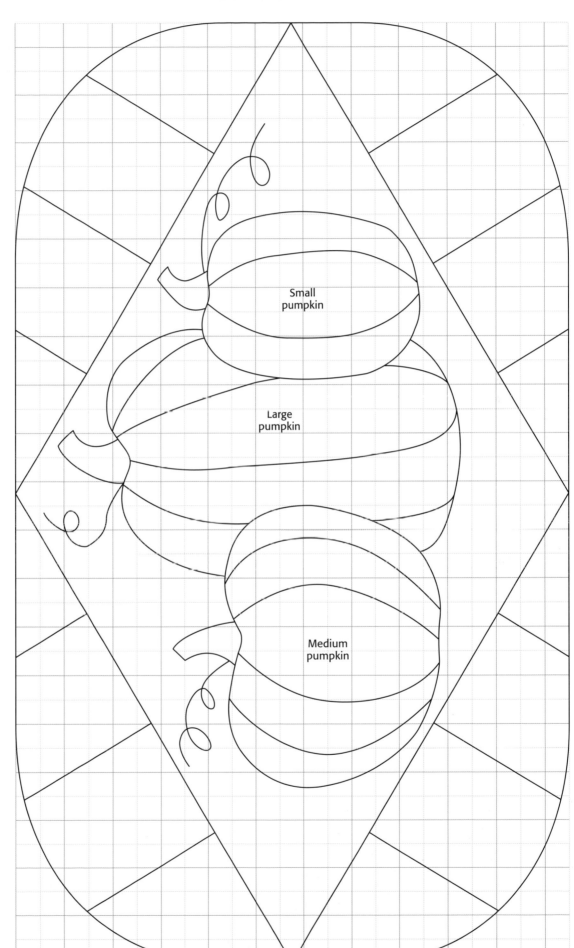

Indian Summer
One square equals ½".
Enlarge pattern 200%
to 11½" x 19½".

Small
pumpkin

Large
pumpkin

Medium
pumpkin

Taupe Garden

Wool Quilt *by Laurie Simpson*

Laurie was inspired by a collection of Japanese quilting fabrics—lovely cotton prints in shades of beige, taupe, rose, brown, and gray—and wanted to use the same color palette for a wool project. The wool appliqué couldn't be easier. She cut all of the shapes freehand—no patterns involved. Laurie encourages you to try the same thing, but if you're more inclined to use a pattern, you'll find them for the flower, the flowerpot, the berries, and leaves following the project directions. However, you'll still be cutting the wavy borders sans pattern!

Finished size: 23" x 35"

Materials

Wool yardage is based on 60"-wide wool (before washing).

- ¾ yard of brown tweed wool for the background

- ¼ yard of olive green wool for the border

- 6" x 24" piece of gray wool for the tongues

- 8" x 8" square of light gray wool for the flowerpot

- 6" x 6" square of salmon wool for the flower

- Scraps of assorted neutral wools for the appliqués

- 1 skein of variegated wool needlepoint yarn for stitching (Laurie used Paternayan 3-ply wool; 4 ounces, 168 yards/skein)

- 30" x 36" piece of cotton fabric for backing/binding

- 28" x 34" piece of cotton batting

- Linen thread

- Embroidery needle

Cutting

Patterns for the flowerpot, flower, leaves, berries, tongues, and pennies are on pages 76 and 77.

From the brown tweed wool, cut:
   1 rectangle, 32" x 23½"; save the scraps for appliqués

From the olive green wool, cut:
   1 strip, 4" x 31"
   1 strip, 4" x 22"
   2 stems: ⅝" x 12" and ⅝" x 17"

From the light gray wool, cut:
   1 flowerpot

From the salmon wool, cut:
   1 of flower piece A

From the assorted neutral wools and leftover brown tweed, olive green, and light gray wool, cut:
   4 stems: ⅝" x 16½", ⅞" x 13½", ¾" x 15½", and ¾" x 17"
   2 stems ⅝" x 16½", cut on the bias
   1 each of flower pieces B, C, and D
   27 large berries
   25 small berries
   9 large leaves
   3 small leaves
   14 large pennies
   3 medium pennies
   11 small pennies

From the gray wool, cut:
   11 tongues

Making the Border

1. Lay the 4" x 31" strip of olive green wool on your rotary-cutting mat and use a rotary cutter to cut a gentle curve through the lengthwise center of the wool. Do not worry about marking the curve; simply cut it freehand. These are the side borders.

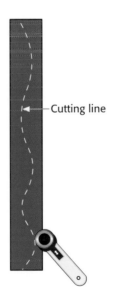

Cutting line

2. In the same manner, cut a gentle curve lengthwise through the center of the 4" x 22" olive green strip to make the top and bottom borders.

3. Arrange the four borders on the brown tweed rectangle to please your eye. Make sure to leave 1" of brown wool extending beyond the green border at the bottom of the quilt, as shown below. Trim away each border end where it overlaps the adjacent border so that the edges will butt up to one another but not overlap.

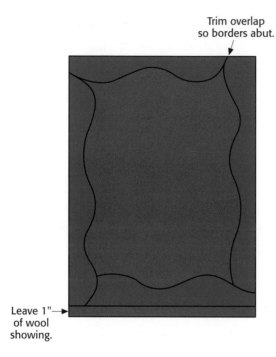

Trim overlap so borders abut.

Leave 1" of wool showing.

4. Baste the borders into place. Using a single ply of the wool yarn, blanket-stitch the top and side border pieces in place along the inside edges. Blanket-stitch all the way around the bottom border.

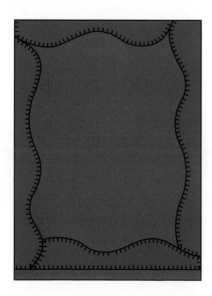

Appliquéing the Quilt Center

1. Arrange the six stems on the center of the quilt top. Baste in place. Position the flowerpot underneath the stems and baste in place. Using one ply of the yarn, blanket-stitch all around the stems and flowerpot. Remove the basting stitches.

2. Blanket-stitch the small berries to the centers of the large berries. Note that two of the large berries won't have centers. Arrange the berries around the stems. Blanket-stitch in place using one strand of wool yarn.

3. Arrange the 12 leaves, referring to the photograph on page 72. Blanket-stitch in place using one strand of wool yarn.

4. Baste the four flower pieces in place, overlapping them. Blanket-stitch in place, working from the largest piece on the bottom toward the smallest piece on top.

5. Stitch the small berries to the larger ones. Notice that in the quilt shown, the three berries that are stitched to the border use short blanket stitches. The remainder are stitched with long blanket stitches that touch in the center of the small pennies to look like spokes on a wheel.

Quilting and Finishing

1. Lay the backing fabric right side down on a table. Smooth out the fabric and tape the corners in place on the table. Lay the batting on top of the backing and smooth it out. Center the wool quilt top, right side up, on top of the batting. Thread or pin baste the layers together. Note that basting spray does not work well with wool.

2. Using the linen thread and an embroidery needle, outline quilt around the flower, the flowerpot, and the border. The hand quilting is done the same way as for a regular quilt, but with a much larger stitch. Echo quilt around the quilting lines to fill in the empty areas.

3. Trim the batting *only* so it is even with the quilt top. Trim the backing fabric so that it is 1" larger all the way around the quilt top.

4. Fold the backing fabric up over the quilt top edge to encase the raw edges of the quilt top and batting. Fold under the raw edge of the backing fabric and whipstitch in place using regular sewing thread.

5. Blanket-stitch around the 11 tongues, leaving the flat ends unsewn. Arrange the tongues with their flat ends butting up to the bottom border of the quilt. Pin in place and then blanket-stitch them to the quilt background fabric along their flat edges.

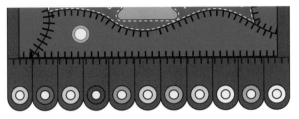

Blanket-stitch tongues with flat edge touching bottom border.

6. For a final touch, use a single ply of the wool yarn and sew a herringbone stitch (see page 15) around the binding edge for decoration.

7. If desired, make a label and hanging sleeve and attach them to the back of your quilt. If you prefer, you can stitch plastic curtain rings to the back of the quilt for hanging.

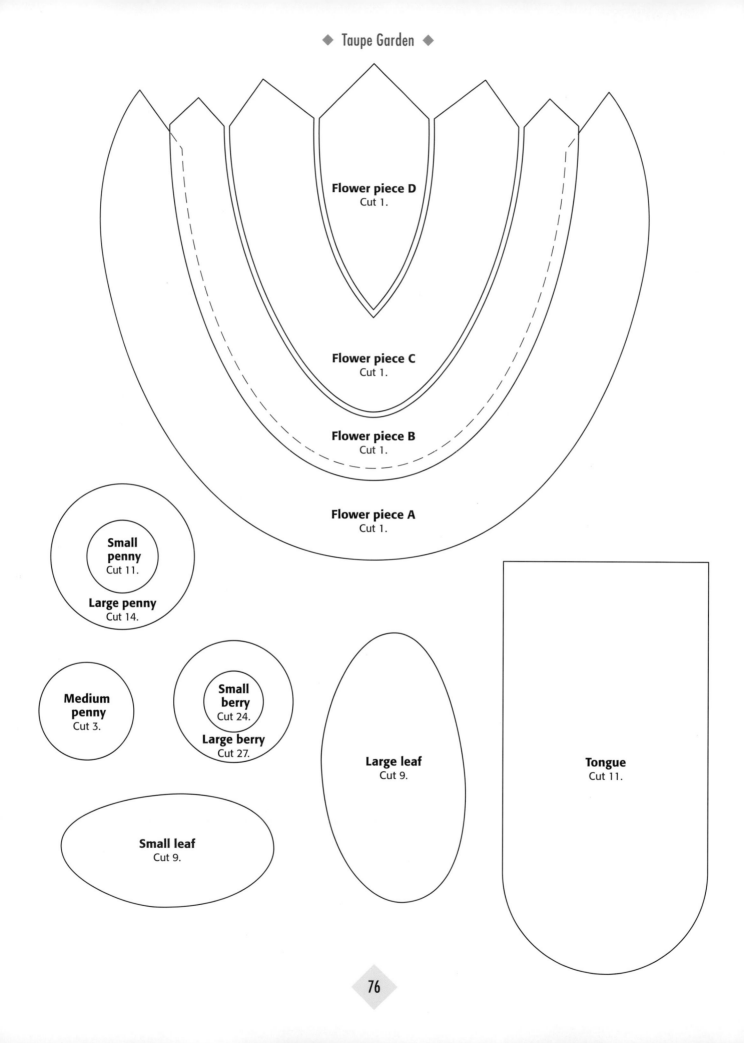

Flower piece D
Cut 1.

Flower piece C
Cut 1.

Flower piece B
Cut 1.

Flower piece A
Cut 1.

Small penny
Cut 11.

Large penny
Cut 14.

Medium penny
Cut 3.

Small berry
Cut 24.

Large berry
Cut 27.

Large leaf
Cut 9.

Tongue
Cut 11.

Small leaf
Cut 9.

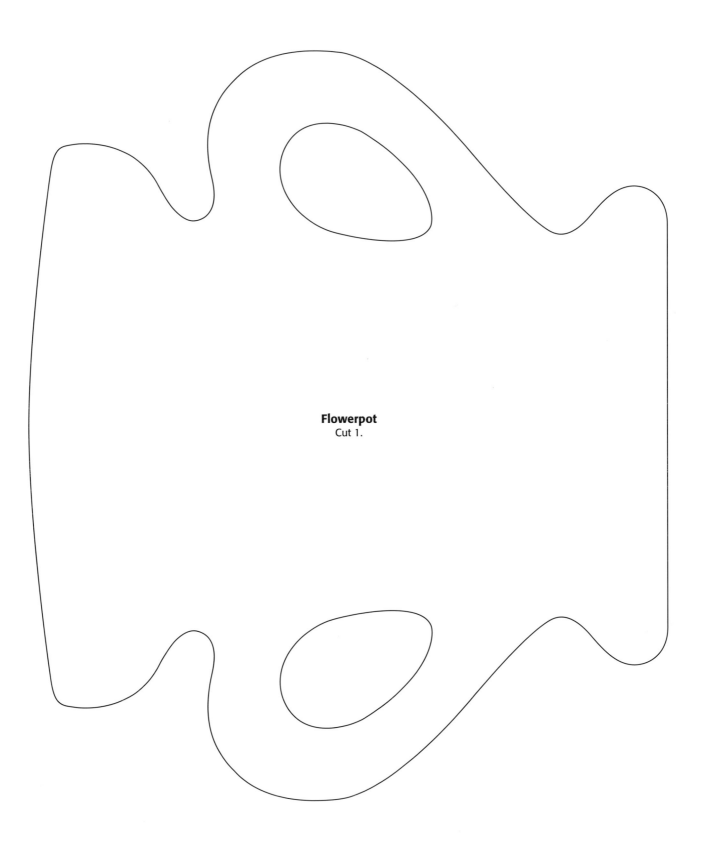

Flowerpot
Cut 1.

Sheep's in the Meadow

Hooked Rug *by Pat Cross*

While overdyeing wools can help you achieve the exact color you're looking for, sometimes using plaids, checks, tweeds, and solids just as they come off the bolt works beautifully. For this rug, Pat chose a neutral-colored plaid for the sheep, and the result is an attention-grabbing speckled fleece. The triangle border is hooked from a more subtle dark green plaid that offers lots of interesting texture at the edges of the rug.

Finished size: 24" x 24"

Materials

Wool yardage is based on 60"-wide wool (before washing). Amounts allow for four times the area to be hooked. Please allow extra wool if you hook high loops or tend to pack your loops close together. This rug was hooked with size 8 strips.

- 1¼ yards of tan wool for the background and bird eye

- ½ yard of dark green plaid wool for the sawtooth border, vines, and leaves

- ¼ yard of grayish green wool for the vines, leaves, and date

- ¼ yard of gray plaid wool for the sheep body

- ¼ yard of blue wool for the sheep eye, bird, and berries

- ¼ yard *total* of assorted red wools for the flowers and berries

- 8" x 18" piece of medium gray wool for the sheep legs and face

- Scrap of charcoal gray wool for the sheep ear

- 32" x 32" piece of rug-backing fabric (40" x 40" if using a hoop)

- 3 yards of black or dark green binding tape

- Red Dot Tracer

- Black permanent marker

Cutting

Cut the assorted wools into size 8 strips. You may want to cut as you go so that you won't risk having your narrow strips tangle together.

Hooking the Rug

1. Enlarge the pattern on page 81 as indicated. Then transfer the pattern onto your rug-backing fabric. For details on transferring patterns, see page 22.

2. Hook the body and ear of the sheep using the gray plaid wool, starting with the outline edge and filling in. Next hook the sheep legs and face using medium gray wool. Hook a blue eye with a starting tail, one loop, and an ending tail.

3. Using both the dark green plaid and the grayish green wool, hook the vines and then hook the leaves.

4. Hook the flowers using the assorted red wools. Also use red wool to hook seven of the berries.

5. Using tan wool, hook the bird eye as you hooked the sheep eye. Hook the bird using blue wool. Hook the remaining five berries with blue wool. Switch to grayish green wool to hook the date.

6. Using the tan wool, outline each motif by hooking one row of loops around the sheep, vine, leaves, berries, bird, and date. Then, using a meandering pattern, hook the background area inside of the vines.

7. If you plan to use binding tape to finish your rug, sew it on now. Hook one row of the dark green plaid wool around the entire perimeter of the rug. Outline the triangles of the sawtooth border and fill them in using the same dark green plaid wool.

8. Hook one row of tan along the edge of the sawtooth border. Fill in the remainder of the background following the contours of the motifs.

Finishing

1. Block your finished rug, referring to page 26.

2. Finish your rug using binding tape. See page 26 for binding techniques.

3. You can add an optional dimensional sheep ear. Use the ear appliqué pattern below to cut a charcoal gray wool ear and stitch it in place over the hooked ear. A couple of stitches, taken at the X as indicated on the pattern, is sufficient to hold the dimensional ear in place.

4. If desired, make a fabric label for the back of your rug and whipstitch it in place.

Ear appliqué pattern

**Alternate date patterns
for hooked rug**

Sheep's in the Meadow
One square equals ½".
Enlarge pattern 200%, and then 167%
(333% total) to 24" x 24".

Hit-or-Miss Footstool

Wooden Stool with Hooked-Rug Top *by Karen Costello Soltys*

My friend Kathy has a wonderful antique hooked rug hanging in her entryway that was made by a Mennonite woman in the 1800s. The rug fascinates me because it was randomly hooked in panels without care or worry about what color butted up to the next. The concept is simple, but the result is dramatic. The little footstool topper shown here is my interpretation of that rug. I used more colors, simply because I had quite a stash of leftover "worms" from previous rug-hooking projects.

Finished size: 17" x 10"

Materials

Wool yardage is based on 60"-wide wool (before washing). Amounts allow for four times the area to be hooked. Please allow extra wool if you hook high loops or tend to pack your loops close together. This footstool topper was hooked with size 8 strips.

Note that the wool amounts are based on completing a rug to fit a 10" x 17" footstool. If your footstool is larger or smaller, then you will need to adjust amounts accordingly. Since this rug is scrappy, the most important adjustment you will need to make is the size of the backing fabric.

- ¼ yard *total* of assorted black wools for border and vertical lines
- Scraps (⅓ yard total) of assorted wools for footstool top (strips do not need to be full length)
- 18" x 25" piece of rug-backing fabric (26" x 33" if using a hoop)
- 3 yards of black rug-binding tape
- Wooden footstool
- 6 small tacks or brads and tack hammer
- Red Dot Tracer
- Black permanent marker

Materials for Finishing the Footstool (Optional)

- Sandpaper
- Satin-finish, water-based black paint, or color of choice
- Wood primer
- 2"-wide paintbrush
- Quilt batting

Cutting

Cut the assorted wools into size 8 strips. You may want to cut as you go so that you won't risk having your narrow strips tangle together. I used leftover strips of assorted colors in assorted lengths. If you are using new wool, instead of hooking with all full-width strips, you may want to cut some of the strips shorter to make your hooking look more random.

Hooking the Rug

1. Enlarge the pattern on page 85 as indicated. Then transfer the pattern onto your rug-backing fabric. For details on transferring patterns, see page 22.

ADAPT TO FIT

If your footstool is not the same size as the one shown, you can easily adapt this pattern to the size needed. Simply trace around your footstool onto the backing fabric to mark the outer edge. (Make sure the footstool is positioned along the straight of grain.) Then mark a line 1" inside the drawn line to create the border. Measure the width of the piece from the left inside line to the right inside line and divide this measurement by five. The result will be how wide you need to make each vertical panel. Using a ruler, measure off each section and mark the backing fabric. Finally, draw a vertical line at each mark to separate the rug into the five panels.

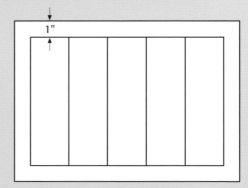

Mark 1" border.
Divide remaining area by 5
to mark vertical lines.

2. Hook the inner border line with black wool. Then hook the vertical lines with black wool. Each vertical line is just one strip wide.

3. Hook one panel at a time. Randomly select a color from your scraps and hook in a straight horizontal line, starting just inside the top border. When you reach the vertical divider line, you can either end the color or turn and hook back. Simply hook until you've used up your strip. Change colors and continue hooking. Notice that some colors happen to end at the black border line while others are long enough to continue hooking a second row. This randomness is what gives the design interest as well as its name—Hit-or-Miss.

4. When all five panels have been filled in, go back and hook just inside the outer border line. Then fill in the rest of the border with black wool.

Finishing

1. Block your finished rug, referring to page 26.

2. Finish your rug using binding tape. See page 26 for binding techniques.

3. If desired, you can paint the footstool. Lightly sand the surface, then paint one coat of wood primer to seal the wood. If your footstool had already been painted and you merely want to change the color, you can skip the primer and simply give it a light sanding.

4. Paint the footstool with two coats of satin-finish black paint, or whatever color you desire. If you purchased an unfinished wood footstool, staining it would also be an option. Allow to dry completely before attaching the rug.

5. Position the finished rug on top of the footstool. Attach it at each corner and along the long sides with small tacks or brads. Simply separate the wool loops with your fingers to position a tack so that it goes through the backing fabric and binding tape only and not through the wool loops. If desired, you can cut one or two layers of quilt batting slightly smaller than the finished rug size and position it under the rug before attaching it to the stool. This adds some padding and extra loft.

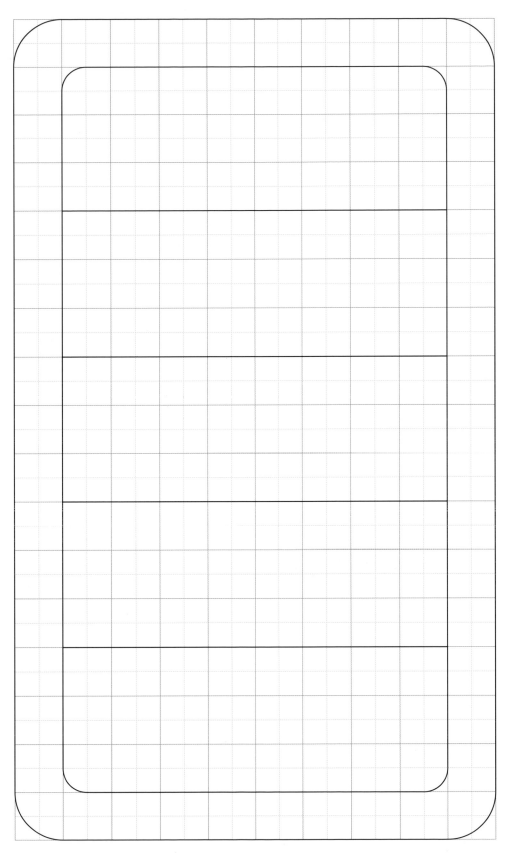

Hit-or-Miss Footstool
One square equals ½".
Enlarge pattern 200% to 10" x 17".

Blue Pot of Flowers

Hooked Rug *by Karen Costello Soltys*

The inspiration for this rug came from a quilted table-runner pattern published in *Romantic Quilts* (Martingale & Company, 2004). I modified the appliqué design, and then added the triangle border, which is reminiscent of borders used on antique rugs. The blue pot is modeled after my collection of blue-decorated stoneware. Part of the fun in making this rug was dyeing much of the wool myself and also trading wool with friends to add both variety and sentimental appeal.

Finished size: 34½" x 22"

Materials

Wool yardage is based on 60"-wide wool (before washing). Amounts allow for four times the area to be hooked. Please allow extra wool if you hook high loops or tend to pack your loops close together. This rug was hooked with size 8 strips.

- ¼ yard *each* of 4 or 5 assorted light wools for the background

- ⅛ yard *each* of at least 6 assorted purple and red-violet wools for the border

- ⅛ yard *each* of at least 6 assorted olive and sage green wools for the leaves, stems, and border

- ½ yard of dusty lavender wool for the blossoms

- ⅓ yard of medium red-violet wool for the blossoms

- ¼ yard of dark purple wool for the blossoms and buds

- ⅛ yard of mottled blue wool for the pot

- 6 to 8 strips of dark cranberry wool for the center flower

- 42" x 30" piece of rug-backing fabric (50" x 38" if using a hoop)

- 1 skein of dark purple wool knitting yarn for finishing edges

- 3½ yards of ¼"-diameter cording

- 3½ yards of rug-binding tape

- Red Dot Tracer

- Black permanent marker

Cutting

Cut the assorted wools into size 8 strips. You may want to cut as you go so that you won't risk having your narrow strips tangle together.

Hooking the Rug

1. Enlarge the pattern on page 89 as indicated. Then transfer the pattern onto your rug-backing fabric. For details on transferring patterns, see page 22.

2. Hook the center design first. Outline the pot and fill it in with blue wool and then hook the flowers and fill them in. Treat each section of the flowers as a unit, outlining it and filling it in.

3. Hook the stems, which are two rows wide. Then outline the leaves and fill them in with the assorted green strips.

4. Fill in the background. First outline each motif and hook one row of loops just inside the border-line. Then fill in the remaining area. In the rug shown, the motifs are echoed with rows of loops until the rows meet. Then the remaining areas are hooked as units, outlining and filling them in to complete the background. See "Instant Antique" on page 88 for more information on hooking a mottled background with a vintage feel.

5. Hook the border. First, outline the interior area of the border in green. Then outline the triangles one at a time and fill them in with assorted green strips. Outline and fill in the purple triangles in the same manner.

Finishing

1. Block your finished rug, referring to page 26.

2. Finish the edges of the rug. The rug shown has cording inserted around the edges that is whip-stitched in place with wool yarn. See page 27 for instructions on making a corded edge. Finish the rug with rug-binding tape.

3. If desired, make a fabric label for the back of your rug and whipstitch it in place.

INSTANT ANTIQUE

I wanted my rug to have an antique look, so even though the background is light, I chose a variety of colors including off-white, oatmeal, cream, yellow, and pale lavender. To achieve the mottled affect, place a bunch of the different colored strips in a basket or bag and randomly pull them out and use whatever color you get your hands on. By not using the colors in any particular order, you'll add lots of visual interest to what would otherwise be a plain background.

Blue Pot of Flowers
One square equals ½".
Enlarge pattern 200%, and then 200% again
(400% total) to 21¾" x 34½".

Resources

Dorr Mill Store
800-846-DORR
www.dorrmillstore.com
Mill-dyed wool

Nolahooks.com
314-966-1813
www.nolahooks.com
Hand-dyed and as-is wool, linen rug backing, hooking supplies, purse handles, and more

Pure Wool
708-601-1979
www.pure-wool.net
purewool@comcast.net
Needle-felting supplies, including needles and dyed wool fleece (roving)

The Red Saltbox
937-847-2162
www.theredsaltbox.com
Hand-dyed wool and primitive linen rug backing

Woodworks Ltd.
800-722-0311
www.craftparts.com
Wood checkerboard pieces: stars and hearts

The Wool Studio
610 678-5448
www.thewoolstudio.com
Selection of as-is wool

Meet the Project Designers

Pat Cross

Pat lives in Charlottesville, Virginia, with her husband and two cats. She has been hooking and designing rugs for 15 years. By using her scrappy or "make-do" style of hooking, Pat makes rugs that look like antiques even though they're made with new rug patterns. She has written articles for *Rug Hooking* magazine, teaches around the country at private workshops and rug camps, and is currently working on her second rug-hooking book, a follow-up to *Purely Primitive: Hooked Rugs from Wool, Yarn, and Homespun Scraps* (Martingale & Company, 2003).

Nola A. Heidbreder

Nola teaches traditional rug hooking and various fiber arts in her home in St. Louis, Missouri, and at rug camps around the country. She has written several articles for *Rug Hooking* magazine and ATHA (Association of Traditional Hooking Artists). Her work has also been featured in Mary Englebreit's *Home Companion* magazine. Nola also does historic craft demonstrations and repairs antique rugs. You can see more of her patterns and find her teaching schedule at www.nolahooks.com.

Linda Lenich and Jennifer Zoeterman of Pure Wool
Linda and Jennifer are inspired by the qualities and possibilities of wool and wool fleece, which led them to create their company, Pure Wool. Linda and Jennifer encourage appliqué artists to use needle felting as a fresh addition to traditional appliqué. Needle felting is quick to learn and easy to do, and adds a dimensional aspect to a needleworker's repertoire. They have written articles for Bernina's *Through the Needle* magazine. For more information about needle felting, wool fleece, felting needles, and patterns, visit www. pure-wool.net.

Tammy Johnson and Avis Shirer of Joined at the Hip
Tammy and Avis have self-published 12 quilt books and over 100 patterns, including their popular Button Up series and Simple Woolens series. They have also designed five lines of fabric. They are coauthors of *Alphabet Soup* (Martingale & Company, 2005) and designers of countless projects that have appeared in various quilting magazines and calendars. They are well known for their primitive, whimsical designs, and love to combine many elements in their quilt designs, including appliqué, patchwork, and traditional quilting fabrics as well as wool, rickrack, buttons, and more to add to the overall charm. For more information about their books and patterns, visit www.joinedatthehip.com.

Donna C. Lever

Making things has always interested Donna. After experimenting with many different crafts—from decoupage to tole painting—she became an avid quilter (with the fabric stash to prove it). As marketing manager for Martingale & Company, she is frequently exposed to many new crafts and claims her job requires her to try them all! Donna has added rug hooking to her list of favorite hobbies.

Wendy Miller of the Red Saltbox

Wendy Miller has been designing rug patterns as the Red Saltbox since 2001. Wendy's rugs have won numerous awards, including the Sauder Award in 2003 and 2005, Heart of Primitive in 2005, and Celebrations XV. She teaches primitive rug hooking seminars at her Red Saltbox studio, which is located next door to her home, a red saltbox-style house. For more information about her studio, seminars, wools, or rug pattern line, visit www.theredsaltbox.com.

Polly Minick

Polly began hooking rugs in the late 1970s when her sons were in high school. Since then, her rugs have become widely known, thanks to stories of her work in various national publications. Articles in *Country Home*, *Better Homes and Gardens*, *Colonial Home*, *Coastal Living*, and *Victoria* magazine have greatly enhanced her status as a folk artist. The *New York Times*, *Houston Chronicle*, and the *Georgetowner* have also written of Polly's achievements. Along with her sister, Laurie Simpson, she has coauthored *Folk Art Friends* (Martingale & Company, 2003) and *Everyday Folk Art* (Martingale & Company, 2005).

Bonnie Smith

Bonnie Smith, publisher of the *Wool Street Journal,* began hooking primitive-style rugs about 13 years ago. She started her quarterly magazine in 2002 for all those who enjoy sharing patterns and ideas for primitive rug hooking. Each issue contains her pen-and-ink drawings as well as articles, patterns, and resources for primitive rug hookers. To her, folk art expressed in the simple design of a hand-hooked rug is the ultimate in heart and hand coming together. Visit Bonnie's Web site at www.woolstreetjournal.com.

Laurie Simpson

For over 30 years, Laurie Simpson has delighted others with her quilts. Her work graces galleries and private collections and has been featured in *Country Home, Coastal Living, Architectural Digest,* and *American Patchwork & Quilting.* A patchwork quilt in a magazine inspired Laurie to take up quilting when she was 14. Drawn to traditional themes and techniques, she pieces, appliqués, and quilts exclusively by hand. "I quilt in the car and at hockey games. Handwork is calming and meditative. It's the way I was meant to work," says Laurie.

Karen Costello Soltys

Karen is an acquisitions and developmental editor with Martingale & Company. She has been sewing since an early age, but started rug hooking only a few years ago. She is one of the original members of the Primitive Chicks, a rug-hooking group that meets regularly in Western Washington to provide inspiration and encouragement to one another. While Karen has had quilts published in several books, the Hit-or-Miss Footstool and Blue Pot of Flowers rug are her first hooked-rug designs to be featured in print.

New and Bestselling Titles from

Martingale®
& C O M P A N Y

America's Best-Loved Craft & Hobby Books®
America's Best-Loved Knitting Books®

That Patchwork Place®

America's Best-Loved Quilt Books®

NEW RELEASES
Alphabet Soup
Big Knitting
Big 'n Easy
Courtship Quilts
Crazy Eights
Creating Your Perfect Quilting Space
Crochet from the Heart
Fabulous Flowers
First Crochet
Fun and Funky Crochet
Joined at the Heart
Little Box of Knitted Ponchos and Wraps, The
Little Box of Knitted Throws, The
Merry Christmas Quilts
More Crocheted Aran Sweaters
Party Time!
Perfectly Brilliant Knits
Polka-Dot Kids' Quilts
Quilt Block Bonanza
Quilts from Grandmother's Garden
Raise the Roof
Saturday Sweaters
Save the Scraps
Seeing Stars
Sensational Knitted Socks
Sensational Sashiko
Strip-Pieced Quilts
Tea in the Garden
Treasury of Scrap Quilts, A

APPLIQUÉ
Appliqué Takes Wing
Easy Appliqué Samplers
Garden Party
Stitch and Split Appliqué
Sunbonnet Sue: All through the Year
WOW! Wool-on-Wool Folk-Art Quilts

LEARNING TO QUILT
101 Fabulous Rotary-Cut Quilts
Happy Endings, Revised Edition
Loving Stitches, Revised Edition
Magic of Quiltmaking, The
Quilter's Quick Reference Guide, The
Sensational Settings, Revised Edition
Your First Quilt Book (or it should be!)

PAPER PIECING
40 Bright and Bold Paper-Pieced Blocks
50 Fabulous Paper-Pieced Stars
300 Paper-Pieced Quilt Blocks
Easy Machine Paper Piecing
Fanciful Quilts to Paper Piece
Hooked on Triangles
Quilter's Ark, A
Show Me How to Paper Piece

QUILTS FOR BABIES & CHILDREN
American Doll Quilts
Even More Quilts for Baby
More Quilts for Baby
Quilts for Baby
Sweet and Simple Baby Quilts

ROTARY CUTTING/SPEED PIECING
40 Fabulous Quick-Cut Quilts
365 Quilt Blocks a Year: Perpetual Calendar
1000 Great Quilt Blocks
Clever Quilts Encore
Endless Stars
Once More around the Block
Square Dance, Revised Edition
Stack a New Deck
Star-Studded Quilts
Strips and Strings

SCRAP QUILTS
More Nickel Quilts
Nickel Quilts
Scrap Frenzy
Successful Scrap Quilts

TOPICS IN QUILTMAKING
Basket Bonanza
Cottage-Style Quilts
Everyday Folk Art
Focus on Florals
Follow the Dots . . . to Dazzling Quilts
Log Cabin Quilts
More Biblical Quilt Blocks
Quilter's Home: Spring, The
Scatter Garden Quilts
Shortcut to Drunkard's Path, A
Strawberry Fair
Summertime Quilts
Tried and True
Warm Up to Wool

CRAFTS
Bag Boutique
Collage Cards
Creating with Paint
Painted Fabric Fun
Purely Primitive
Stamp in Color
Trashformations
Vintage Workshop, The: Gifts for All Occasions
Year of Cats…in Hats!, A

KNITTING & CROCHET
200 Knitted Blocks
365 Knitting Stitches a Year: Perpetual Calendar
Classic Crocheted Vests
Crocheted Socks!
Dazzling Knits
First Knits
Handknit Style
Knitted Throws and More for the Simply Beautiful Home
Knitting with Hand-Dyed Yarns
Little Box of Crocheted Hats and Scarves, The
Little Box of Scarves, The
Little Box of Scarves II, The
Little Box of Sweaters, The
Pleasures of Knitting, The
Pursenalities
Rainbow Knits for Kids
Sarah Dallas Knitting
Ultimate Knitted Tee, The

06/05